Small Talk

Unlocking the Hidden Power of Casual Conversations to Forge Authentic Connections and Elevate Your Personal and Professional Life

Free Bonus from Andy Gardner

Hi!

My name is Andy Gardner, and first off, I want to THANK YOU for reading my book.

Now you have a chance to join my exclusive email list related to human psychology and self-development so you can get the ebook below for frcc as well as the potential to get more ebooks for free! Simply click the link below to join.

P.S. Remember that it's 100% free to join the list.

Access your free bonuses here:
https://livetolearn.lpages.co/andy-gardner-small-talk-paperback/

Table of Contents

INTRODUCTION 1

CHAPTER 1: THE ART OF SMALL TALK 3

CHAPTER 2: THE MAGIC OF FIRST IMPRESSIONS 12

CHAPTER 3: THE IMPORTANCE OF LISTENING 21

CHAPTER 4: HONESTY AND AUTHENTICITY 33

CHAPTER 5: EMBRACING DIVERSITY THROUGH SMALL TALK............ 41

CHAPTER 6: NETWORKING AND PROFESSIONAL SMALL TALK........... 50

CHAPTER 7: NAVIGATING SOCIAL ANXIETY 63

CHAPTER 8: THE ART OF BODY LANGUAGE 72

CHAPTER 9: EASING INTO DIALOGUE (WHEN IT TERRIFIES YOU)...... 84

CHAPTER 10: MOVING FORWARD 94

CONCLUSION 103

HERE'S ANOTHER BOOK BY ANDY GARDNER THAT YOU
MIGHT LIKE 105

FREE BONUS FROM ANDY GARDNER 106

REFERENCES 107

Introduction

Small talk is one of the greatest arts of civilization. It lays the groundwork for effective communication. It's the basis of all kinds of talk. The term was first coined sometime in the 18th century, but people have been engaging in small talk since the dawn of civilization. It may not serve any practical purpose, but it's a crucial social skill without which you cannot proceed to a meaningful conversation. It's like a knock on the door of a room filled with treasures. That knock may not make any difference in your life, but it opens the door to something far more valuable.

This book will teach you how to master small talk to open the treasure trove of engaging conversation. You'll start by understanding the importance of this art and going over its basic rules. Is it really possible for anyone to engage in small talk? Can even the most reserved person master the art?

As they say, the first impression is the lasting impression. Does it hold true for small talk, too? How can you make the best first impression while staying true to yourself? Then, you'll come across an interesting paradox: the art of listening. Aren't talking and listening two different things? What does small talk have to do with listening? As it turns out, quite a lot!

It has much to do with talking, too, but you won't get very far without honesty and authenticity, as you'll learn in another chapter. Also, it won't help if you are too judgmental or not particular about diversity. Do you often make statements about stereotypes?

Once you master the art of general and inclusive small talk, you'll be led into the fascinating world of small talk in the workplace. There are many similarities between social and professional small talk, but there are quite a few differences.

By then, you may have understood everything about small talk, but do you still struggle to master it? Is your reserved nature or social anxiety keeping you from taking the first step? You'll learn how to overcome all your social problems and fears as you step into finer aspects of small talk, like body language, and take your conversation to the next level.

This book is easy to understand, even if you are a non-native speaker. The language is simple, and the examples are highly relatable for a diverse audience. The well-researched and carefully curated content is perfect for both introverts looking to find ways to open up and extroverts hoping to refine their small talk skills.

Chapter 1: The Art of Small Talk

Have you ever been to a party but felt left out because you didn't know how to initiate a conversation? Do you feel anxious thinking about how you'll get through another networking event when you don't know what to talk about? You are not alone. We have all been there. Making small talk and leaving a good impression on the other person is an intricate skill that most people wish they were taught in school. But that's okay. It is a quite learnable skill, which will be discussed in great detail in this book.

How do you view small talk? If you dread just thinking about it but feel that it is necessary to make an impression and create deeper connections, then you're like most people. At networking events, do you want to cut to the chase and jump right to the point? Do you wonder why some feel it's important to waste time talking about the weather or the latest game? Well, these little interactions are necessary and can act as building blocks for stronger relationships.

Small talk can completely transform your personal and professional life.

If you learn to accept and enjoy small talk, it can help to completely transform your professional and personal life. These few moments can open up a bundle of new opportunities for you in all spheres of life. It can help you get that promotion you've been eyeing for a while, make a great first impression on a first date, and even help form friendships at parties. Chit-chat is the key to potentially beautiful relationships and deep conversations. Avoiding this chatty part of interaction inhibits our chances of creating meaningful connections. Not engaging in casual conversations at networking events or parties may even cause you to come off as disinterested or rude, and that can seriously harm your chances of getting that new job, promotion, or relationship.

Small talk consists of three parts:

Having an Ice Breaker:

First, to engage in small talk, you must have a good ice breaker. This will help you initiate the conversation and establish a ground for continuing the conversation.

Building Rapport:

Rapport is where you ask further questions regarding their response to continue the conversation. This shows that you are interested in learning about them and what they have to say.

Having an Exit Strategy

Having an exit strategy is also really important. You must know when to end the conversation gracefully and take yourself out of the situation.

It is just as crucial as the conversation itself, as leaving the conversation abruptly may leave a bad impression on the other party.

If you want to become a great conversationalist, then you must learn the art of small talk. But, before that, you have to first understand why small talk matters.

Why Small Talk Matters

This part of the conversation has many wonderful benefits. It has already been established how these casual bits help people to accelerate their personal and professional lives. But how does it affect your life in the broader spectrum? Let's take a closer look to see how these small moments help shape the course of your life.

Health Benefits

Research indicates that these small interactions have a positive effect on your health and well-being. The little moments of connection with strangers help boost your happiness. An article published at the Harvard Business School reports that having conversations with your colleagues, a clerk at the grocery store, or your Uber driver builds relational diversity. It is a unique predictor of well-being. Moreover, one meta-study explored how people with great social lives were 50% less likely to die during the study period than those who did not have such a strong social network. This study was true for both introverts and extroverts.

The Perfect Mood Booster

Small talk can boost your mood.

https://unsplash.com/photos/a-woman-sitting-at-a-table-in-front-of-a-window-S_YOuAUMm2o?utm_content=creditShareLink&utm_medium=referral&utm_source=unsplash

Small talk can help you feel like you belong to a community. It boosts your confidence and trust in others. Simply chatting with a stranger on your ride home or greeting a passerby on your daily walk can help improve your mood. In an experiment conducted by Gillian Standstorm, the participants who had conversations with the barista while placing their order reported having a stronger feeling of belonging and an enhanced mood. Small talk often promotes learning and expands your worldview. It is also useful for both parties to engage in the conversation. According to research, people view minimal social interaction, such as a compliment, a smile, or a quick chat, as an act of kindness.

Keep an Open Mind and Don't Assume the Worst

When it comes to chatting with strangers, people tend to think that their efforts will not be reciprocated. They assume the worst about such situations, which makes it hard for them to socialize. Their fear of the conversation going badly prevents them from realizing their full potential. "What if they reject me?" "What if they don't want to talk to talk to me?" These are thoughts that haunt most people, but it is comforting to know that people are turned down a lot less than you may think. According to Standstorm, people are turned down only about 10% of the time, and that is because the other person may be stressed or preoccupied with something else. Also, sometimes you may think that you'll have a better time keeping to yourself. But, studies suggest otherwise. One research instructed commuters in Chicago to either strike up a conversation with their fellow commuters or keep themselves to themselves. The results reported that the people who had assumed that they would enjoy being by themselves had a more positive experience interacting with other commuters. No matter what that critic in your head may say, studies suggest that people actually like others more than they think they do.

Among other benefits, small talk helps people find shared interests and common ground with others and often catalyzes strong relationships with others. Moreover, it also helps to improve your active listening skills and makes you a better listener, teaching you that you have much to learn from others and that you'll learn better if you pay close attention to what people tell you. Small talk helps reduce social anxiety as well. The more you engage in these casual conversations with strangers, the better your spontaneity will get and help you overcome your social discomfort. Plus, if you want to form better bonds with people, this part of interaction lays the foundation for you to create that psychological safety that is required before having deeper and more vulnerable conversations.

Can Anyone Small Talk?

It may seem like small talk is only for extroverts, but that is far from reality. Small talk expert Gillian Standstorm, who enjoys making casual conversations with strangers herself, identifies as an introvert. Making small talk with strangers is an art, and anyone can learn it, whether you're an introvert or an extrovert. These conversations usually occur at important social events or parties and are important for establishing rapport with others and getting to know them better. People use small talk to reduce discomfort and ease into social situations. You may be considered rude if you jump onto personal questions about someone regarding work or family life. This is why starting conversations with broader topics (like the weather) is necessary; then, get to the specifics as the conversation develops.

Strategies to Make Small Talk

At one point or another, everyone will find themselves in the middle of such situations, and your only weapon of choice will be making small talk. Here are some strategies to help make small talk in any situation.

Take a Deep Breath

If you're feeling nervous about starting a conversation, then take a long and deep breath. You'll have better conversations if you're feeling relaxed. Have confidence in your ability, and don't worry about making mistakes. You risk losing sight of the discussion and coming across as disinterested if you obsess over what you have to say next. Focusing on the other person and attentively listening to them will help calm your nerves. Also, make sure you keep the conversation positive and don't focus too much on the negatives. Compliment the food or the music. Appreciation and gratitude will reflect better on you.

Open-Ended Questions Are the Best

Asking open-ended questions rather than specific ones is the best strategy to begin small talk. This leaves room for the conversation to flow naturally and take the conversation forward. Most people feel comfortable talking about things they know about rather than things they don't know. For example, asking people about themselves will likely lead the conversation in a positive direction. People will have a hard time following if you ask them a really specific question about some sport they know nothing about rather than a simple "Which sport do you enjoy the most?" Open-ended conversations generate dynamic conversations and motivate the other person to open up.

Engage in Active Listening

People can tell when you're not paying attention to what they are saying. Your disinterest in them will cause them to close down. It may also make you come off as rude. Active listening also helps you to create stronger relationships. If the other person notices that you seem interested in what they have to say, then they will enjoy talking to you more. You'll also be able to ask relevant, more detailed questions at a later time if you listen attentively.

Put Away Your Phone

This one goes without saying, but it is important to put your phone away when you're talking to someone, especially if it's your first time talking to them. Looking at your phone while trying to strike up a conversation with someone is a perfect recipe for an awkward encounter. People sabotage their chances of holding meaningful conversations by trying to find comfort in their phones. If you're too distracted by your phone, people may not reach out to you because they think that you're busy. You'll also seem disinterested if you're too immersed in your little electrical box!

Be Enthusiastic

Many people fear small talk, but if you embrace it and go into it with the right mindset, then you may even end up having a lot of fun. You can learn a lot from others, even in a few minutes of conversation. View small talk as an opportunity to learn about other viewpoints and other people. People are full of surprises. You never know what you'll end up learning or what the other person will be open to sharing. You must always look forward to having wonderful conversations that may be in store for you.

The 10 Rules of Small Talk

Like everything else in life, there are some rules to having effective small talk as well. It can make or break your relationship with others. This is why knowing what to do and what not to do is important. Here are 10 rules of small talk that you must follow in order to have a more meaningful impact on others.

1. Intruding or Interrupting an Ongoing Conversation Is Never a Good Idea

One of the worst things you could do at a social event is to interrupt an ongoing conversation. This is not only against basic etiquette but will also make you look like someone who cannot read the room. If you see two parties engage in a conversation, then it is probably not a good time for you to intrude. Timing is everything. You must first wait for the conversation to quieten down. You can jump in once you have their attention and ideally receive a non-verbal cue from them (like "Hi, there!" or "Hey, what do you think about..."). You should also keep distance in mind. Do not stand too close or too far away. A healthy distance will help you get heard, and you should avoid speaking too loudly or too quietly.

2. Don't Speak if You Have Nothing to Say

If someone appears to be thinking or lost in their own thoughts, it is best to ask them for permission before talking to them. Try starting your conversation with, "Hi, can I talk to you for a second?" rather than going into their personal space and interrupting them abruptly. Also, make sure you have a question or a comment in mind. A question like, "Are you having a good time?" usually works well. It is all about making the situation comfortable enough for the other person to respond.

3. Avoid Controversial Topics

Controversial topics such as politics hardly ever make for good icebreakers. Such topics tend to divide people, and you're better off not starting a conversation in the first place! You never know how someone new will respond to a weighty, off-putting topic like this. You can let the conversation flow toward such topics naturally, but it is best to stay away at the start. To initiate conversations, you can go for a simple subject, something that you and the other person can comment on together. It could be anything ranging from music to food or even decor. In this way, you'll both be able to connect more easily.

4. Skip Questions about Marriage, Kids, and Work

When you're trying to strike up a conversation with a stranger or an acquaintance, it is best not to talk about any potentially sensitive topics. Asking someone if they are married or have kids as a conversation starter may not be taken well. Similarly, asking someone what they do for a living may not be such a good idea either. You do not know their current employment status, and it is possible that that person may not feel comfortable disclosing it. (It's also an oft-overused conversation starter.) You can be creative and try another more general topic that may not come off as too inquisitive. For example, you can ask something like, "If you could go back in time and do one thing, what would it be?" Such questions put the other person in charge of the conversation and may even lead to a deeper conversation.

5. Make Sure That You're Easy to Follow

Once you have established a connection with each other, make sure to keep that connection going by being easy to understand. If you both speak different languages, try to speak slowly and clearly. Make it easy for them to hear and understand you properly. Moreover, if you have a habit of talking in slang, try eliminating it from the conversation because they may not understand you. It will create a divide between you if you use words or jargon that they may not be able to grasp. If they ask you a simple question like what you do for a living, try responding in a manner that will be easy for them to follow.

6. Do Not Talk Too Much about Yourself — or Them

It is often said that people love talking about themselves, and they enjoy it when you ask them follow-up questions. However, this may not be true for everyone. Not everyone likes talking about themselves, and if you feel the other person is feeling interrogated, _stop_ asking questions and share an experience of your own instead, or offer your opinion on the subject being discussed. You can take the limelight off them by shifting the conversation to yourself. To ensure that they enjoy the conversation as well, you can ask them questions about anything new that you've learned, such as the new restaurant in town or your favorite author, etc.

7. Do Not Waste Anyone's Time

If you have engaged someone in a conversation, talk directly with them. Staring at the floor or looking at something else may not be the best idea. Try to stay present and give them all your attention. Otherwise, the other person may feel you're not interested in talking to them or wasting their time. Small talk may seem inauthentic or unimportant, but it is the key to forming strong relationships. Being fully interested in what the other person has to say will go a long way.

8. Use Body Language to Establish Rapport

Body language is one of the most powerful aspects of a conversation that people often forget. You can use your body language throughout the conversation to show how interested you are. Visual cues are essential when it comes to showing the other person that you are actively listening to them. Making eye contact and passing an assuring smile will go a long way. Only smile if the topic being discussed is not of a serious nature. You must maintain open body language. In other words, do not cross your arms or fidget during the conversation. Also, stay focused on the speaker and do not look around the room to see what others are doing. Nodding and "humming" agreement during the conversation goes a long way, too.

9. Don't Expect Too Much

Do not go into the conversation with too many expectations. You will not make friends at every social gathering, which is completely fine. Don't pin too much hope on every interaction, as it may discourage you from engaging in casual conversation with strangers. Embrace each opportunity with open arms, but do not expect anything from it. You may become best friends or never meet again. The conversation can go either way, and that's okay. You learn something from every meeting, and that should be your only goal.

10. Finish on a Note of Gratitude

Ending a conversation may seem difficult if you are new to learning the art of making small talk. Debra Fine, a leading researcher, advises that it is best to end the conversation with gratitude. You must thank the other person for their time. Telling them you enjoyed the conversation will go a long way toward endearing them to you. Expressing gratitude will boost your chances of creating a lasting relationship with them as it will leave the other person feeling good about themselves. If you are interested in connecting with that person again, you can simply send them an email or text or make a phone call to them within a day or two.

Chapter 2: The Magic of First Impressions

Your ability to make a great first impression can make or break your intention to form a connection with someone through small talk. You only have one opportunity to do this, and less than a minute at your disposal. Underscoring the significance of initial encounters in shaping perceptions and future interactions, this chapter dives into the psychology of first impressions, offering a glimpse into the conscious and subconscious factors that influence people's judgments of others at that first meeting. It also highlights the role of non-verbal cues, authenticity, and the lasting impact of those initial moments on personal and professional relationships.

First impressions can decide whether or not a connection will form.

The Psychology Behind First Impressions

As a quintessential element of human interactions, first impressions have interested scientists and philosophers since ancient times. It has long since been established that how people view a person's internal traits is determined by their very first interaction with them. One of the oldest theories comes from Aristotle, who claimed that one can learn a great deal about another person's character by looking at their facial features.

A Swiss pastor named Johann Kaspar Lavater also took an interest in this topic in the late 18th century, his publications describing the ability to read a person's face to learn their character as physiognomy. According to his theory, it is possible to tell whether someone is suited for a job simply based on their features like the width of their forehead or the shape of their nose. Delicate features were associated with intelligence, while rough physical traits and expressions meant the person belonged to the working class. However, this didn't take into consideration fleeting emotions, which people often display through facial mimics during interactions with others.

During Darwin's explorations, he also took note of how those he met on his travels reacted to first impressions. While most of his journals spoke about native peoples' reactions to facial features and expressions, Darwin also mentioned using Lavater's theory to gain advantage and favors from those he traveled with. As he described, on one occasion, he had to assert that he was an adventurous person to a ship captain who didn't want to let him travel on his vessel. It turned out that the captain, who was also a believer of Lavater's theory, upon taking one look at Darwin, decided that someone with Darwin's nose couldn't possibly have sufficient stamina to take the voyage they were about to embark on. However, after being convinced and proven wrong by Darwin (who not only withstood the trials and tribulations of seafaring life but also incorporated it into his research), the captain was pleasantly surprised.

While early research on the psychology of first impressions focused solely on physical traits, modern studies are more geared toward the concept of first impression bias and the role of first impressions in various cultures and disciplines. The former is also associated with the confirmation bias and the halo effect (first described by American psychologist Edward Thorndike in 1920).

When considering the traditional impact of first impressions, people's cultural, socioeconomic, and learned beliefs all play a role. In many cultures, people judge each other based on shared ideas rather than what impression they give during the first meeting. Even in a professional setting, they're more likely to let a poor first impression slide if it belongs to a person of the same culture than they would with a person who doesn't share their tradition. People in Chinese societies, on the other hand, form opinions of those they meet based on the person's competence in one or more areas of life. In other cultures, physical strength plays a similar role, while in a third cultural group, it is social status.

A person's first impression can influence others to place more weight on information they received about them beforehand than on what the person will convey later. In practice, this means that if a person hears that you possess a specific negative trait (like shyness, awkwardness, etc.) and you display this trait during the first 30 seconds of meeting them, they'll confirm this information, and you'll find it hard to change their mind. Even if you manage to overcome these traits, break the ice, and engage with them later, their first impression of you will be forever tainted by those first seconds.

The *halo effect* is a long-term implication of an extremely positive first impression. This is a superb example of what makes people believe beauty equals intelligence. From social media to job interviews, this unique effect of first impressions can be seen everywhere in today's world. A well-groomed, stylishly dressed person is more likely to be hired for high-paying jobs, even if their skills and experience don't reflect desirable traits – a decision that often ends up costing the employer a lot more than anticipated. In another example, a hiring manager may feel a connection with a candidate (for example, because the candidate is wearing the emblem of the sports team the manager is rooting for). In just a few minutes after establishing the connection, the manager is won over by the candidate's charisma and determines that the candidate will be just as hardworking as he is. In reality, the candidate may have very little experience and be unsuitable for the job – but seeing the connection, they were able to leverage their charm to land the job.

Confirmation bias also plays a critical role in developing first impressions. While it can have even more negative consequences (for example, it may lead researchers to incorrect conclusions when trying to confirm a hypothesis), it's also much worse than the halo effect. When confirmation bias happens, a person only looks for information that concurs with their existing beliefs and dismisses any conflicting notion. Its power lies in its long-term impact on interpersonal connections. For example, a person may come up with an idea for a new business, convinced they can successfully convert their hobbies into a lucrative source of income. They ask friends and relatives to invest in their business, encouraging them to look into the idea and do their research. They present the idea enthusiastically, radiating positive authenticity, and everyone believes them. However, when the business fails, those who've lost their money realize their impression was wrong because everything they did was based on the person's own conviction of their success.

Nowadays, people's attention spans are getting even shorter, and it takes mere seconds for them to judge a person's trustworthiness in both professional and personal areas of life. It takes another few seconds to form a precise and often unchangeable conclusion about the person's competence and personality. This snap judgment will endure, *even though it doesn't accurately describe the other person.* Unfortunately, it's easy to make a negative first impression. However, when it gets ingrained in people's minds, you'll have to work very hard to change their opinions. Snap judgment is linked to the halo effect because both rely on the perceived qualities and resulting belief. Accordingly, learning how to make a good first impression to avoid both is recommended. By increasing your chances of making a positive impression, you can make connections with more ease. Likewise, if you make an authentic first impression, you can avoid getting into situations that lead to disappointment and strain your relationships.

By using effective impression-management techniques and abilities, you'll be able to avoid the pitfalls of making the wrong first impression. However, to do this, you must be aware of how you come across to others when meeting them for the first time. By hiding characteristics that are known to create a poor impression and focusing on strengths that will make you look confident and authentic, you can create a more favorable opinion of yourself in the eyes of others.

The Power of Non-Verbal Communication

People's opinions about one another are based on several factors, including vocal inflection, facial expressions, perceived emotional state, and attractiveness. Besides the attention to the vocal cues, the rest are nonverbal. These often hold much more power than how the person conveys information verbally. Because a large chunk of the first impression comes from nonverbal cues, how you smell, sound, and look communicates much about you when meeting someone new.

Facial expressions can cause people to form opinions.
https://www.pexels.com/photo/woman-wearing-pink-top-1036620/

Besides these sensory stimuli, people also pay attention to body language. Much more than the words you utter, a person will form an impression of you based on how similar your behavior is to theirs. It's no secret that people prefer to be surrounded by those with similar attitudes, personalities, beliefs, and looks. Suppose you meet someone new, and your body language is very different from theirs. In that case, they're likely to form a negative impression of you.

Facial impressions are particularly crucial when forming an opinion of someone. Studies of how people develop preferences in today's world show that an opinion can be made in as short a time frame as 33 milliseconds at the first meeting. (Palomares et al., 2018). It takes a mere glance at a person's face, and based on their expression, an impression is formed instantly.

Another factor that affects nonverbal communication and first impressions is the belief that others share commonly accepted opinions. People often think more people share their ideas and values than they actually do. Whether they can confirm their belief when meeting someone or not will influence their opinion about this person. Suppose this person demonstrates their differences right away. In that case, the first impression can easily become a negative one, whereas if they do indeed share beliefs (or act as they do), both parties are more likely to form positive impressions of each other. Besides spoken words, people often rely on nonverbal cues to determine whether someone shares their beliefs. For example, if someone speaks about the shared interest animatedly, using open gestures and warm facial expressions, they convey that they share the other person's beliefs and are likely to be perceived positively.

Sometimes, people's behaviors at the first meeting result in being ascribed qualities they don't possess. For example, suppose someone walking into a job interview appears unsure and out of place. In that case, the interviewer will immediately form doubts about the person's competence. The candidate may possess all the qualities they need to fulfill the role but lack confidence in themselves, and, even worse, they're displaying it for the world to see. Similarly, if a candidate walking into a job interview appears arrogant, they're just as likely to receive a negative first impression. The worst part is the person may not even realize they look or act arrogantly – they're only displaying traits arrogant people do, so the interviewer immediately thinks they are arrogant too!

Facial symmetry is likely to affect first impressions, too. If a person has symmetrical proportions, they're more likely to leave a positive first impression as they'll be thought of as trustworthy, intelligent, and kind. However, if someone only acts in a way that conveys symmetry (for example, smiling makes a person's face more symmetrical, as opposed to a hostile expression, which contorts one or more parts of the face), this can also be perceived as positive A symmetrical face will also make the person seem more approachable and attractive. So, you see, when making a first impression, it's critical to use non-verbal communication the right way so the opinion will be a positive one. Although changing someone's mind after they form a negative perception of you isn't impossible, you can easily avoid having to do it by using the right nonverbal cues, saving yourself from a lot of hard work later on.

Nonverbal communication is particularly vital in forming first impressions in a professional setting. For example, when two people meet to establish a business partnership, they'll judge each other on the other's posture and hand gestures, facial expressions, eyebrow position, and frequency of eye contact. If both begin the conversation with a firm handshake, leaning toward each other but keeping their posture straight, displaying a warm smile, and looking firmly into each other's eyes, they're more likely to reach an agreement regarding their partnership.

This type of positive attitude can help you form positive first impressions in other facets of life. It's a tool that can easily influence how others see you. Bringing positive energy to your interactions makes it far more likely for others to form a favorable opinion of you. Likewise, if you're meeting someone who, based on their nonverbal cues, seems optimistic in the first few seconds you meet them, you'll be more likely to see them as a positive person you'll be able to count on.

Being Authentic: Why Genuine Connections Start at Hello

Your voice will also affect people's judgment of you. When you meet someone for the first time, they'll begin to form an impression of your personality as soon as you utter the first syllables. Certain words have a bigger impact on this process. This was confirmed by a study (McAleer P. et al., 2014) that measured how people reacted to the word "hello." In this study, people were asked to read a paragraph containing the word, and their voice was recorded. Then, the parts where they uttered "hello" were isolated from the recordings and played back to a large group of volunteer participants. This group was asked to rate the voice of the other group based on a range of personality traits, including warmth, trustworthiness, dominance, aggressiveness, and confidence. The research found that people usually formed the same impression of the voices and the personalities they imagined behind them. For example, they all voted one of the male voices particularly untrustworthy because they sensed it instilled fear. The voice had a much lower pitch than the voices that were considered trustworthy. The researchers theorized that this was likely because people tend to associate high-pitched voices with traditionally feminine traits like warmth and friendliness rather than male traits like aggression. Additionally, they found that female voices that drop at the end of the word are felt to be more trustworthy as they also convey a lack of aggression, whereas female voices that were raised at the end of the word were considered less trustworthy.

The study above shows just how easy it is to convey the right impression by simply saying hello in the right way. By the time you have finished this word, those who heard it have already made a snap judgment of your personality. Based on how you're perceived after uttering these words, others will decide whether to approach you or not.

One of the easiest ways to make a positive first impression from the moment you say hello is to convey authenticity. This characteristic resonates deeply with most people because no one likes to be surrounded by people who display fake emotions. After all, this is seen as a sign of manipulative behavior. Authenticity, on the other hand, conveys that the person is who they say they are. Being your unapologetic self is also liberating for you because it makes evoking the right first impression (and making small talk) so much easier.

Raising your self-awareness can help you become more authentic in your communication. When you understand and embrace your goals, values, and ideas, you can convey them honestly in words and actions. Remember, being authentic also means being honest, which goes a long way toward building trust with a person you've just met. People are very good at spotting when someone is portraying something they're not.

Authenticity entails showing sincere emotions, even if it makes you uncomfortable. Showing vulnerability creates empathy and an instant bond with others. At the same time, it's also critical to respect others' authenticity. Respecting a person's differences from the first time you meet them conveys that you're able to embrace diversity, which encourages an open and genuine conversation. Being authentic doesn't only mean embracing your strengths and imperfections but also these qualities in others.

When people notice you're being your authentic self, they're more likely to follow suit. The reason behind this lies in people's innate tendency to mirror and match the verbal and nonverbal cues of those with whom they interact. While people often tend to do this when conversing with someone who shares their beliefs and opinions, you can evoke this reaction by being open and honest when making the first impression. It's a powerful way to instill a sense of connection within the other person/people.

Naturally, the key to conveying authenticity is subtlety. Blurting out controversial opinions could have the opposite effect. When hearing opinions that radically differ from the prevailing one in a given social circle, people will think you're trying too hard and being insincere. Look at people's reactions and match your style to theirs.

The best way to be your authentic self is to begin a conversation with a warm greeting. After hearing their name, repeat it by saying, "Hello, (the person's name), it's nice to meet you." However, don't use the person's name too many times in the conversation that follows. Doing so could make you look insincere. Recall and repeat their name once more to show you care enough to remember. This conveys a genuine wish to form a deeper bond with them (it seems authentic because most people strive to create connections with others).

Showing authenticity always makes your interactions more enjoyable and memorable. While it may seem like a small gesture to many, to be seen as your authentic self has a substantial impact on leaving a great first impression.

As its name implies, an authentic smile is another tool to show you're truly being yourself during conversations. This is a universally accepted sign of approachability and trustworthiness and an immense help when building bonds and leaving lasting impressions. After all, who would you rather have a conversation with? Someone who shows authentic interest in you by smiling and showing excitement about your conversation topic or with someone who, while seemingly willing to engage in the conversation, keeps a forced facial expression? An authentic smile involves not only the muscles around the mouth but around the eye, too. Suppose you have wrinkles at the corner of your eyes when smiling at them. In that case, your conversation partner will be assured that you're showing genuine interest. Authentic smiling also implies that you know when to smile. Smiling at inappropriate times conveys insincerity and is the easiest way to provoke a hostile reception, which can soon lead to awkward silences and a premature end to the conversation – not to mention a terrible first impression.

Authenticity is a fundamental part of an attractive smile. At the same time, smiling sincerely shows you have a positive attitude. People who tend to leave lasting positive impressions always think positive thoughts before approaching someone, ensuring their smile reflects their authentic warm feelings and makes them seem friendly and approachable.

Chapter 3: The Importance of Listening

Listening is a fundamental and often underestimated skill pivotal to human communication and relationships. It is the process of not just hearing words but actively paying attention and comprehending the message being conveyed. Effective listening is more crucial than ever in a world filled with noise and distractions. It serves as a cornerstone for many parts of our personal and professional lives and, when done properly, offers many benefits.

Listening is a pivotal skill in human communication.

By truly listening, anyone can understand their surroundings better, foster meaningful connections, resolve conflicts, and gather valuable information. Listening enables individuals to empathize, learn, and collaborate effectively, making it an indispensable tool for building strong and harmonious relationships and achieving success in various endeavors. Nevertheless, recognizing and embracing the importance of listening is essential for personal growth and interactions with others.

The Difference between Passive and Active Listening

Intent and Purpose

When it comes to passive listening, intent and purpose are minimal or absent. When you're listening passively, your primary goal is to receive general auditory information, often without any specific aim. You may be present in a situation with sounds or conversations, but you're not actively trying to make sense of them or engage with the content.

On the other hand, active listening is a purposeful and intentional act. When you actively listen, your primary intent is to engage with the speaker's message, understand it, and gather useful information. You actively seek to comprehend and participate in the conversation.

Attention and Focus

In passive listening, your attention and focus are usually low. You may be in a state of mind where you're easily distracted and not actively trying to concentrate on the speaker or the information being conveyed. Your focus could be scattered, and you could be thinking about other things or simply allowing your senses to register the sounds around you passively.

Conversely, Active listening requires your full and undivided attention. You consciously concentrate on the speaker's words, tone of voice, and non-verbal cues. Your mind actively processes the information, and you make a concerted effort to understand what's being said.

Information Retention

Information retention in passive listening tends to be limited. Since your intention and attention are low, you may not need to remember what you've heard quickly. Your brain processes the information minimally and doesn't get committed to your memory for long.

On the flip side, information retention in active listening is focused. Actively processing and engaging with the content helps improve your memory and understanding. You are more likely to remember and internalize what you've heard.

Engagement and Feedback

Passive listening rarely involves any form of interaction or feedback. You're a passive information receiver and do not actively engage with the speaker. This means you're likely to refrain from asking questions, providing responses, or actively participating in the conversation.

However, active listening encourages interaction and feedback. You actively participate in the conversation by asking questions, providing verbal and non-verbal cues demonstrating your engagement, and offering thoughtful responses. This dynamic interaction leads to a more meaningful and productive dialogue.

Empathy and Understanding

In passive listening, empathy and understanding are not often engaged. You may not connect with the speaker's emotions or perspective. You're more of an observer, not deeply considering the speaker's point of view or feelings.

However, active listening involves empathy and a sincere attempt to understand the speaker's perspective. You actively work to connect with the speaker's feelings, emotions, and points of view. This empathetic approach can lead to stronger interpersonal relationships and more effective conflict resolution.

While passive listening is a more inert, superficial, and less engaging form of receiving information, active listening is a skillful, proactive, and intentional approach that fosters effective communication, understanding, and empathy. It involves heightened attention, engagement, and an active effort to connect with the speaker's message, ultimately leading to improved relationships and better communication outcomes.

Attentiveness in Listening

Genuine attentiveness is a powerful tool that significantly enhances interactions with others and encourages deeper, more meaningful connections. Here's how.

Building Trust

Imagine you're having a conversation with a close friend who's going through a tough time. You decide to be genuinely attentive, listening to their worries, fears, and frustrations. Your friend feels heard and validated by you, demonstrating that you're fully present and engaged. This helps build trust because they know you care about their well-being. In the future, they are more likely to turn to you for support, knowing that you're a reliable and empathetic listener.

Enhancing Communication

Consider a professional scenario where you're in a meeting with colleagues. You practice genuine attentiveness by actively listening to their ideas and concerns. Your colleagues notice your engagement and appreciate that their opinions are valued. This results in a more open and collaborative work environment. People are more willing to share their thoughts and engage in constructive discussions, leading to better decision-making and problem-solving.

Strengthening Personal Relationships

Think about a family gathering where you are genuinely attentive to your loved ones. As you listen to their stories, concerns, and dreams, you create a deeper emotional connection. By showing that you're there for them, you strengthen your bonds. This enriches your family relationships and creates a sense of security and support that everyone can rely on.

Resolving Conflicts

When a conflict arises with a friend, you are genuinely attentive during the conversation. You actively listen to their grievances and perspectives, demonstrating empathy and understanding. This approach de-escalates the tension and opens the door to productive conflict resolution. Your friend feels heard and validated, making finding common ground easier and reaching a mutually satisfactory solution.

Empowering Others

Picture a mentoring relationship where you, as the mentor, practice genuine attentiveness with your mentee. By actively listening to their aspirations, concerns, and challenges, you empower them to set and achieve their goals. Your support and guidance are informed by a deep understanding of their needs, which boosts their confidence and personal development.

Creating Lasting Impressions

Suppose you're meeting someone for the first time at a networking event. You leave a lasting positive impression by genuinely attending to what they say and asking thoughtful questions. Your interest and engagement make them feel valued, increasing the likelihood of them remembering and wanting to connect with you.

Genuine attentiveness is a relational skill that strengthens trust, communication, and emotional connections in diverse aspects of life. It empowers individuals, fosters empathy, and promotes constructive interactions. Actively listening and engaging with others can create more meaningful and fulfilling personal and professional relationships.

The Psychological and Emotional Underpinnings of Active Listening

Effective listening is not merely a surface-level skill but is deeply rooted in a human being's psychological and emotional makeup. Understanding these foundations can provide valuable insights into why active listening is so powerful in building meaningful connections and communication.

Empathy

Effective listening is underpinned by empathy.
https://www.pexels.com/photo/ethnic-psychologist-touching-black-depressed-clients-shoulder-5699491/

Effective listening is often underpinned by empathy, the ability to understand and share the feelings of another. When you actively listen, you hear the words spoken and strive to grasp their emotional content. You create a profound emotional connection by empathizing with the speaker's emotions and experiences. Empathy demonstrates care and understanding, making the speaker feel valued and validated.

Trust and Safety

Listening effectively creates a sense of psychological safety. When someone feels genuinely heard and understood, they are more likely to trust the listener. Trust is essential for open and honest communication. Trusting that the listener will not judge, interrupt, or misinterpret what is being said encourages individuals to express themselves more freely.

Validation

Active listening provides validation, which is a fundamental human need. Listening attentively signals to the speaker that their thoughts and feelings are valid and vital. This validation boosts self-esteem, affirms their sense of self-worth, and strengthens the emotional bond between the listener and the speaker.

Reducing Anxiety and Stress

Knowing that someone is genuinely attentive can reduce anxiety and stress. When individuals feel heard, they articulate their concerns more lucidly and find relief in sharing their burdens. Effective listening helps to alleviate emotional distress, creating a positive and supportive environment.

Conflict Resolution

Effective listening plays a crucial role in conflict resolution by addressing the emotional aspects of disagreements. Actively listening to both parties' perspectives, the listener can identify the underlying emotions contributing to the conflict. Acknowledging these emotions and demonstrating understanding can de-escalate tension and pave the way for rational problem-solving.

Connection and Belonging

Deep listening builds a sense of connection and belonging. Every human craves a connection with others. When anyone feels heard and understood, they experience a sense of belonging, which is fundamental for emotional well-being.

Enhanced Communication

Emotionally, effective listening enhances communication by allowing the speaker to express their feelings and thoughts more clearly. When individuals feel their emotions are acknowledged, they are better equipped to articulate their ideas and needs, leading to more effective and productive conversations.

Increased Self-Awareness

Effective listening is not just about understanding others; it can also increase self-awareness. You'll become more attuned to emotions and reactions. This self-awareness can lead to personal growth, improved emotional intelligence, and better self-regulation.

Positive Feedback Loop

Active listening creates a positive feedback loop. When individuals experience effective listening, they are more likely to reciprocate by doing the same in return. This mutual exchange of active listening will deepen emotional connections and create a supportive, nurturing environment.

The psychological and emotional underpinnings of effective listening are closely tied to empathy, trust, validation, and creating a safe, understanding space. Active listening enhances communication and contributes to emotional well-being, conflict resolution, and the establishment of deep, meaningful connections with others.

Tips and Techniques for Active Listening

It's often said that speaking makes people heard, but listening makes others feel seen and understood. Effective listening is a transformative skill that enriches personal and professional relationships. Here are some techniques and habits to help you become a more attentive listener.

Give Your Full Attention

Giving your full attention means making a deliberate choice to focus entirely on the person who is speaking. This means physically and mentally clearing away distractions. Turn off your phone or place it face-down, close any open computer screens or books, and remove any objects that might divert your attention. By doing this, you create a dedicated space for the speaker, showing them that their words are your priority.

Maintain Eye Contact

Eye contact is a potent non-verbal cue that communicates your engagement and interest. Keeping eye contact with the speaker creates a connection and shows that you are present in the conversation. It signals that you are actively listening and are interested in their perspective. It's essential to be mindful of individual and cultural differences regarding eye contact and adjust your approach accordingly.

Practice Mindfulness

Mindfulness is a mental state of being fully present in the moment, without judgment or distraction. While listening, mindfulness involves consciously immersing yourself in the speaker's words, tone, and body language. To do this, let go of your thoughts and resist the urge to think of responses while the other person is speaking. Mindfulness lets you feel the nuances and emotions behind the words so you'll be able to respond more effectively.

Avoid Interrupting

Interrupting the speaker disrupts their flow and can be seen as dismissive or disrespectful. Effective listening requires restraint and the ability to hold back your thoughts and responses until the speaker has finished speaking. Allow them the space to express themselves fully, even if it means waiting for a pause in their speech. This shows respect for their viewpoint and creates an open and honest dialogue environment.

Use Non-Verbal Cues

Non-verbal cues are a powerful tool for conveying your attentiveness without words. These cues may include nodding to signal agreement or understanding, smiling to express encouragement, or using affirmative gestures like a thumbs-up or a supportive hand on the shoulder. These non-verbal cues reassure the speaker that you are actively engaged and receptive to their message.

Ask Open-Ended Questions

Open-ended questions encourage the speaker to give you more extensive and detailed responses. They cannot be answered with a simple yes or no. Asking questions like, "Can you tell me more about that?" or "How did that make you feel?" invites the speaker to share more deeply and express their thoughts and emotions more fully.

Reflect and Clarify

Periodically, take a moment to reflect on what you've heard to ensure you've grasped the speaker's message accurately. This reflection may involve paraphrasing or summarizing what the speaker has said. Phrases like "If I understand correctly, you're saying..." or "Could you clarify what you meant by..." show that you are actively processing the information and trying to comprehend it accurately.

Be Patient and Non-Judgmental

Patience in listening means letting the speaker express themselves at their own pace. Avoid rushing them or pressuring them for information. It's also essential to approach the conversation without judgment. Suspend any preconceived notions or opinions. Being non-judgmental creates a safe and open environment for the speaker to communicate honestly without fear of criticism or condemnation.

Cultivate Empathy

Empathy is the ability to understand and share the feelings of another. To cultivate empathy in your listening, try to put yourself in the speaker's shoes. Pay close attention to their emotions, needs, and perspective. Show a genuine willingness to understand their experiences, and avoid making the conversation about your own experiences. By doing this, you connect with the speaker on a deeper emotional level, demonstrating that you acknowledge their feelings and perspectives.

Stay Curious

A curious mindset means approaching each conversation with a genuine interest in the speaker's words and experiences. It involves an eagerness to explore their thoughts, feelings, and perspectives with interest and an open heart. Curiosity fuels engaged and attentive listening. It encourages you to ask questions and seek to understand the speaker's viewpoint in greater detail.

Practice Active Listening

Active listening is an advanced form of listening that goes beyond passive hearing. It involves techniques such as paraphrasing or summarizing the speaker's words, asking clarifying questions to confirm understanding, and providing feedback during the conversation. These active listening techniques reinforce your commitment to comprehending the content and demonstrate your genuine engagement in the dialogue.

Self-Reflection

Self-reflection is the process of periodically examining your listening habits and identifying areas where you can improve. It involves developing self-awareness regarding any potential barriers to effective listening that you may possess, such as impatience, judgment, or distractions. Self-reflection helps you recognize patterns in your listening behavior and allows you to make adjustments over time to become a more attentive and responsive listener.

Silence Your Inner Monologue

Effective listening requires silencing your internal dialogue. Avoid thinking about how you'll respond, planning what to say next, or forming judgments or opinions about what the speaker is saying. This way, you free up mental space to fully engage with the speaker by quieting your inner monologue.

Practice Mirroring

Mirroring is imitating the speaker's body language and tone.

Mirroring involves subtly imitating the speaker's body language and tone. This creates a sense of connection and empathy. If the speaker is sitting relaxed, mirroring their posture conveys that you are attuned to their emotions and experiences.

Control Your Body Language

Your body language can speak volumes about your attentiveness. Sit or stand in an open and receptive posture, avoiding crossed arms or other defensive stances. Maintain an open facial expression to demonstrate that you are approachable and engaged.

Respect Pauses and Pacing

Pay attention to the natural pauses in the speaker's speech and their pacing. When someone hesitates or takes a moment to gather their thoughts, respect this by allowing a pause without interrupting. This shows your patience and understanding of their need to articulate their ideas in their own time.

Avoid Offering Unsolicited Advice

While it's tempting to jump in with solutions or advice, the speaker sometimes just needs to be heard. Avoid offering unsolicited advice unless it is explicitly sought. People often appreciate having a sounding board for their thoughts and emotions before moving to problem-solving.

Manage Your Reactions

Be aware of your emotional reactions to the speaker's words. If you get emotional, remember that the focus should remain on the speaker. You can acknowledge your own feelings while still providing space for the speaker to express themselves without being overshadowed.

Check Your Assumptions and Biases

People all carry assumptions and biases that can influence their listening. Practice introspection to identify any preconceived notions that affect your ability to hear what the speaker is truly saying. Acknowledging and challenging these assumptions can make you a more open and impartial listener.

Validate Feelings First

When the speaker expresses strong emotions, it can be helpful to validate those feelings before delving into problem-solving or analysis. Phrases like "I can see that you're upset about this" or "It sounds like you're feeling overwhelmed" show that you understand and acknowledge their emotions.

Practice Reflective Listening

Reflective listening involves paraphrasing what the speaker has said to demonstrate your understanding and engage in a deeper level of dialogue. For example, you might say, "So, if I'm hearing you correctly, you're feeling frustrated because..."

Follow-up and Check-in

Effective listening doesn't end when the conversation does. Follow up with the speaker later to check on their well-being, ask if they need further support, or inquire about the progress of their situation. This demonstrates that you genuinely care and are committed to their concerns.

Adapt Your Listening Style

Recognize that different individuals have varied communication styles. Some prefer direct and concise conversations, while others appreciate more emotional or detailed discussions. Adapt your listening style to suit the person who is speaking to you to create a more comfortable and practical exchange.

Provide Space for Silence

Silence can be a powerful tool for compelling listening. Allow silence during the conversation, especially after the speaker has shared something meaningful or emotional. This silence provides space for reflection and demonstrates your willingness to receive and absorb what has been said.

Incorporating these tips and techniques into your listening habits can improve your ability to make others feel seen and understood. Remember that becoming an attuned listener is a continuous learning process that requires mindfulness, self-awareness, and a commitment to nurturing deeper connections and relationships.

Chapter 4: Honesty and Authenticity

Social anxiety, especially regarding communication, rears its head when you overthink your responses to cater to what you think a group wants to hear. Once you delve into your head too much and morph your words to create an identity that does not match who you are, your inauthenticity will be easily noticeable. When you speak with a voice that is not yours, inevitably, you'll awkwardly stumble through a conversation, tripping up on simple exchanges. Trying to hide your natural quirks will only increase your awkwardness because your conversational style will seem derived, robotic, and manufactured.

You must accept the reality that not everyone will like you or agree with your opinions. The killer of authenticity is when you do not try to connect but instead aim to conform to an uncomfortable mold. People intuitively pick up when someone is playing a character. They may not immediately identify the mask, but after some time, they will notice that you are not being true to yourself. Once people feel you are inauthentic or dishonest, they are unlikely to open up to you because you have proved that you are untrustworthy.

If you are dishonest, people will be unlikely to open up to you.
https://www.pexels.com/photo/text-5981542/

The social mask you wear may not be intentionally crafted to deceive. Nonetheless, the outcome of taking on false identities is deceptive and misleading. Hiding your authentic self often comes from insecurity and a lack of self-esteem. You need to realize that you are worthy of taking up space and that your social contributions hold as much weight as anybody else's. Live in your truth and embrace the entirety of your being, including the embarrassing parts. You can embody the permission people need to express themselves freely because your vulnerability encourages others to let their guard down, too.

Truthful Doesn't Mean Hurtful

Many people use honesty as a bludgeoning bat to tear down people. Being a so-called "blunt" person has become a code word to let people know they can expect dismissive rudeness. Honesty does not have to be handcuffed to being impolite. You can be mindful of your words and tones while still affirming your truthful opinions and perceptions. Open and clear communication while considering the next person's feelings is how you can be truthful but not hurtful. It can be difficult to walk the fine line between being honest and being compassionate, but a cheat code that can assist you in finding the balance is considering how you would want someone to talk to you if they were unhappy.

People who have trouble communicating honestly and openly often do so because they are afraid of hurting the feelings of someone who has upset them. This bottling up of emotions does not help strengthen relationships but rather does the opposite by breeding resentment. Jeff is married to Jennifer. He consulted a therapist because it felt like there were two extremes of communication occurring in his marriage. Jeff felt that his wife was not fulfilling their agreements about the household regarding bills and chores. Jeff was taking on the bulk of the financial responsibilities as well as the majority of the chores in the home. Jeff responded to this perceived imbalance either by holding his tongue and letting it go or by yelling and insulting his wife.

Through the therapeutic process, Jeff learned that he did not need to resort to verbal aggression to get his point across. Jeff spoke about how he felt about Jennifer and reinforced what they agreed on. Furthermore, Jeff asserted boundaries by stating what he was willing to do and what duties he would no longer take on because they had agreed that Jennifer would do them. With this gentle yet firm communication, they were able to strengthen their marriage simply by changing how they spoke and engaged with one another. Jeff was honest about how he felt but avoided blaming and attacking language when addressing the issues he had in his marriage. With firm boundaries, clear communication, and consideration for the next person's opinions and feelings, you can be honest without being hurtful. You do not have to invalidate anyone to feel validated. Instead of using language that shifts the focus into attack like "You make me angry," rather use language that centers yourself like "I feel angry because..."

Authenticity without Oversharing

Oversharing is when you divulge information about yourself that is too personal or inappropriate for the individual you are sharing it with to hear. For example, you can tell your doctor about the unknown growth that you have on your private parts, but it will be extremely weird if you tell that to a stranger you met at a bus stop. It is difficult to determine where the line for oversharing what is private for some is no big deal for others, meaning the definition of oversharing is subjective. To determine the difference between *oversharing* and *being authentic,* it is best to use consent.

Before you open up to somebody about personal details of your life, it helps to ask if they are comfortable or okay with hearing the information. This will stop you from including unnecessary information in a conversation, and the practice of getting consent shows that you respect the person you are talking to. This is especially important when discussing difficulties in your life or trauma you've experienced. You never know what can be triggering for someone who is listening to you, so being mindful of how they will receive the information you exchange is crucial to building powerful connections. You don't want to find yourself in the space of dumping your trauma onto someone when it could be emotionally draining for them.

There are many reasons people overshare. Someone may be trying to rush an intimate bond, they may be avoiding anxiety, or it could be a way to avoid awkward silences. Suppose you look at oversharing as a consequence of social anxiety or as an eagerness to connect. In that case, there are some steps you can take to protect yourself from participating in this sometimes self-destructive activity. One simple tip that seems like common knowledge but is often forgotten is to think before you speak. Being socially anxious can drive in uncontrollable rambling to alleviate the discomfort of an unfamiliar social scenario. Therefore, slowing down and thinking about your words can prevent you from getting caught in the trap of rambling.

Not oversharing does not mean you are being inauthentic. You do not have to change who you are as a way to stop oversharing. Being mindful of which information is appropriate to share is all about understanding social cues. Observe people's body language to determine whether you are saying too much. If you doubt whether you are capable of installing the filter that takes out information that is too personal, you can stick to asking questions to prompt the other person to speak. By asking questions, you can gauge what the next person is comfortable sharing and follow their lead.

Moreover, remember people can use personal information against you. Therefore, if you share anything private with someone you do not know well, be aware of the ways it can be used to your detriment. Context is everything, so your surroundings and the position of the individual you are talking to will act as a guide to what should or shouldn't be said. You do not have to hide who you are, but you should be selective of what layers of yourself you share with others. People need to dig deep to get the diamonds, but there are flowers available on the surface that anyone can pick.

Building Authentic Friendships

From a young age, people have a more positive self-image if they feel like they are being authentic. Even if you get people to buy into the crafted idea of yourself, you'll eventually experience discomfort and instability that is a result of functioning outside of a true expression of yourself. Authenticity is a vehicle for connection that can function in real-time to make new friends and establish the bonds that facilitate lifelong relationships.

Trent was an introvert who had a few close friendships. His friends often encouraged him to go out to parties and social events with them, but he often refused because he felt awkward. In the town where Trent was from, his interests (cartoons and anime) were very niche, so he used the internet as his main way to find connections. Talking to people face to face was intimidating for him because he constantly worried that his niche interests would make people think he was weird.

One of his friends told him that he should stop overthinking his conversations and instead openly talk about what he likes. He highlighted to Trent that the worst that could happen is that the person he is talking to would not be interested in the same things he loves, which would either cause the conversation to end or they could move on to a new topic. He emphasized that Trent had nothing to lose by expressing himself. Trent took his friend's advice and mentioned to someone he met at a party that he enjoyed anime and cartoons. Surprisingly, the woman he spoke to enjoyed the same kinds of things. She was glad to have met Trent because not many people in their town were into the same thing. She showed him tattoos of cartoon characters that she had, which excited Trent a lot. They established a strong friendship based on their shared love of cartoons and often met up to attend conventions and events together after they had met.

By being yourself, you open pathways to meet people who are on the same vibe as you. When you fake it, you attract people who do not necessarily align with the values, principles, and interests that you have. Your friendships will, therefore, be built on a shaky foundation because the people you interact with fall in love with a character you are playing instead of liking you for who you are. It is better to be hated for who you are than to be loved for something you are not because, at the end of the day, you'll start hating yourself because you'll feel as if the real you is not good enough to be appreciated.

Connecting Through Vulnerability

Many people walk around with a hard shell built from the negative experiences they have had. Lowering those barriers is difficult because it makes it more likely that you'll get hurt. Using vulnerability as a tool for connecting applies to many kinds of relationships. For example, if a leader opens up to their team about their sensitivities, the team will be in a better position to achieve their goals because they know the shortcomings and insecurities of the leader. Furthermore, this can prompt the team to also share their weaknesses or soft spots. Now that the team is more transparent, they can work from a more informed place and cater to one another by filling the gaps that others are unable to reach.

Vulnerability is foundational to establishing and maintaining relationships; it means opening yourself to being harmed either emotionally or even physically. When it comes to communicating, this characteristic takes the form of sharing your emotions, especially if they are negative, like fear, sorrow, or anxiety. Being vulnerable isn't just oversharing. Rather, it is expressing yourself truthfully with emotional transparency so that there is a rope of humanness for someone to grab onto. The opposite of vulnerability is *isolation*. Every person experiences low moments, so behaving as if you are always at the top of your game all the time will lead to you becoming more isolated because you are hiding your possible weaknesses from the world.

The nature of vulnerability requires you to take on some risks because people could take advantage of you or belittle your feelings when you express them openly. However, the risk is worth it because being vulnerable makes it much easier to bond. Imagine you were standing in a line heading toward an epic rollercoaster ride at a theme. You initiate a conversation with the person behind you in the line. If you tell your line neighbors that you are nervous and terrified to get on the ride, they may relate to your openness and honesty. Rollercoasters are meant to be scary, so the chances are they are also scared. This negative feeling of fear is transformed into a bonding experience that can be used to build a friendship.

The reason that many celebrities share their life stories on social media is to create a sense of familiarity with their supporters by giving people a glimpse into their private lives. This online communication requires a level of vulnerability because the celebrity is sacrificing their privacy. This sacrifice pays off because if their fans feel more connected to them, they are more likely to support them. The same is true when you meet new people. If you show your imperfections, flaws, and concerns, owning them proudly, you build more trust because you are demonstrating your honesty by being emotionally transparent.

Shattering Your Social Mask

Social masks feel protective, but they slowly corrode your true essence. Nobody is the same person all the time. The person you are to your parents is probably not the same as the person you are to your employer. Similarly, the person you are at work is most likely not the same as who you are when you go out with friends to have fun. These different versions of yourself are all a distortion of the true you that you keep hidden deep within. Breaking your social mask is not about getting rid of all the contextually relevant versions of yourself, but it is rather getting all your faces to match your core values as closely as possible. In other words, do not allow the social shifts in your identity that inevitably occur with interactions to betray the core of you or to do anything that would conflict with your real self.

Shattering your social mask is about being comfortable in your skin. Embrace your differences. The flavor of the individual that you are will not match everyone's taste, but you still have to serve up the dish that is you unashamedly. To take off the social mask you hide behind, you need to internalize the harsh reality that not everyone will like you, and there is nothing you can do about that. The people who don't match with you are not the ones you'll bond with strongly. Your ability to connect is reserved for those who resonate with you and share common values, principles, goals, and interests.

Embracing Yourself

The foundation of connection is vulnerable honesty and authenticity. Being authentic is the essence of staying true to yourself. Before you go out to establish any relationships, you must first be secure in yourself. How you define yourself will determine the kinds of relationships you pursue and the types of people with whom you aim to bond. Furthermore, when you are solid in your identity with high self-esteem, it makes you magnetically attractive to people around you.

Although authenticity and being yourself do not automatically ensure positive outcomes in life, they will make your internal experience more bearable because you are your primary critic. When your motivation comes from your authentic self, meaning the truest reflection of your emotional and mental state, your action will align with your desire. If being true to yourself yields negative social, psychological, and emotional results, the issues you need to address are more apparent, so even in your detrimental behavior, you gain awareness of what you need to change, which can never be uncovered when you hide from the truth.

It is natural to want to present yourself in the most favorable light. People want to put their best foot forward, especially around new groups, so their first impression can be lasting. However, when you act like someone you are not, you often disappear into the crowd because you are mimicking generic behavior that people deem as good. Admitting that you have shortcomings and advertising your strengths proudly is beneficial because you reduce the anxiety of having to put up too much of a front. When your anxiety and stress levels are higher, it will reflect in your mannerisms and tone of voice and can reduce your overall effectiveness. Therefore, you are better off uplifting yourself so you can be calm enough to present yourself optimally, especially if it is the first time you meet a person.

If you analyze high-level athletes, they constantly practice so that their performance in the game can become second nature. At the highest levels, the only difference separating the greats from the average is their ability to perform well under pressure. If you are pretending to be someone you are not, when pressure knocks at your door, you'll more than likely slip up because your mind is distracted by playing the role you have chosen. There is no pressure to hold up appearances when you are being yourself, so you can respond in a free-flowing way that is not held back by the constraint of acting.

Chapter 5: Embracing Diversity through Small Talk

Through socialization processes, humans develop implicit biases. As a social species, people have in-group biases and prejudices against people they identify as outsiders. People subconsciously hold discriminatory perceptions borne of misunderstandings and a lack of effort to learn about anything outside of their tribe. As you move around the world, particularly in bigger cities, you'll encounter people from different backgrounds. Conversation becomes a conduit of intercultural understanding through which all the parties involved gain a deeper understanding and appreciation of the differences diversity brings. You do not have to agree with every opinion or practice, but by reaching out to those far outside the boundaries of your comfort zone, you'll find that you can learn a lot from different frameworks and models of the world.

Small talk can help you embrace diversity.

https://www.pexels.com/photo/group-of-people-standing-indoors-3184396/

Prejudice stems from mystery. People fear what they are unfamiliar with. Assuming that the rustle in the bushes is a dangerous predator rather than the wind is a lifesaving instinct of evolution because it is safer to expect the worst. However, when you take a look at what's behind the bush and find that there is no danger, you can relax. Realizing your prejudices and taking the journey, using small talk to address them, broadens your horizons, giving you a more comprehensive view of society and the world. The world has become smaller because communication and travel technology have advanced to incredible heights. Diversity is unavoidable, so for the benefit of humanity, it is essential to learn to live and work together. Effective small talk and openness give you an alternative lens through which to view reality. By sharing your experiences and opinions with others, you'll find out that you have so much to offer, but, just as importantly, you'll see that you can learn a lot from those who are different from yourself.

Is Small Talk a Universal Language?

All humans around the world are social and connect by talking. Although small talk will take culturally specific forms, using language and expression as a way to connect is universal. Some cultures are more openly expressive, wearing their emotions on their sleeves, while others tend to be more reserved. There are region and group-specific ways to engage, so it helps to be aware of who you are talking to. What is seen as perfectly acceptable for one group may be a rude insult for another. Luckily, in the modern era, it is easy to do research in preparation for meeting people whose culture is unfamiliar to you. If you don't get the opportunity to research a new culture, you could encounter small talk as the perfect tool to learn the etiquette of people from different backgrounds. Your desire to connect will be felt regardless of any cultural stumbles you might make along the way.

As it is traditionally defined, small talk is not embraced by all people. For example, in Germany, it is uncommon for people to casually discuss anything that is not work-related in the office. Trying to force small talk in such an environment may be alienating, creating distance from people around you. In places where small talk is not as common, it takes a little longer for relationships to form. Therefore, it is good to remember that your conversation will not always be received the same way, but that does not mean people do not like you. Imagine attempting to have casual talks about how your weekend went in an office full of people who don't see the point of this kind of conversation in the workplace. It will seem as if people hate you, and pushing the engagement more forcefully will not help your case.

So, do not narrow your view of small talk, but understand that the goal of your conversation is to connect. If you find yourself among people who do not use small talk as the predominant way to build bridges, you can find other ways to reach out to them. For example, in heavily collectivist cultures like Korea, a gesture such as bringing snacks to a group meeting could be received well. Putting the carriage in front of the horse by forgetting the purpose of small talk puts you at a disadvantage. Conversation aims to facilitate a common ground for mutual acceptance, so if people are not open to small talk, you can embrace other strategies to reach out. Context and setting also play a part in how small talk is received. For example, in Japan and China, meeting up for drinks after work is where people loosen up a little so they are willing to talk more openly in a non-professional setting. It is best to function within the social constraints of the common culture you find yourself in to see the most effective ways to connect and in what instances small talk is appropriate.

Understanding Diverse Cultures, Backgrounds, and Experiences

Communication across thousands of miles and geographical borders is instant in our current world. Moreover, journeys that were treacherous, taking months across rough seas, are now cut down to hours with a slightly annoying wait at the airport. In these conditions, understanding diverse cultures, experiences, and backgrounds is essential for social cohesion and establishing new relationships. When you grow up in a relatively homogenous environment where most people around you have similar experiences and share overlapping points of social reference, it is easy to forget that not everyone is the same as you. From the food you eat to the games you played as a child and even the holidays you celebrated, all seem so ingrained that you neglect that those experiences could have been completely different for the next person.

There is a famous quote from the freedom fighter and former president of South Africa, Nelson Mandela, that says, "If you talk to a man in a language he understands, that goes to his head. If you talk to him in his language, that goes to his heart." The spirit of this quote can extend beyond the point about language that Mandela was making to include participation in all cultural activities because when you show interest in what is meaningful to others, it shows that you are open to receiving them. It would be difficult to learn every language, but you can bond over food, clothing, entertainment, or regional interests. For example, football, ice hockey, basketball, and baseball are huge sports in the United States, but they do not have the same global appeal as soccer. Asking someone in India who their favorite basketball player is will probably not be as impactful as asking them who their favorite cricket player is. Therefore, learning about different cultures gives you the key ingredients to connect in an increasingly diverse world.

Your views have been influenced by how you grew up. Speaking to people about their cultural experiences and the principles they hold will give you an entirely new outlook that allows you to question what you have been taught. The only way to progress is to break free from the boxes that you were put into, which necessitates peeking through the slits in the cardboard. By understanding the variety of identities that surround you get to see and know new realities that you never knew existed, which opens up new worlds for you. Instead of having the mindset of framing cultures as better or worse, be open to seeing them simply as different, like red or blue. You may not want to paint your room red, but it is not the end of the world if someone else does. Similarly, you do not have to abandon your traditions and beliefs to respect other cultures.

Cross Cultural Appreciation, Sensitivity, Curiosity, and Respect

The primary basis for mastering small talk is to establish bonds with emotionally, socially, and financially beneficial people. This goal is completely demolished once you offend people or treat them with cold disregard. Therefore, cultural appreciation, sensitivity, curiosity, and respect are essential components of communicating in the context of multiculturalism. Cultural sensitivity is the awareness that there is not one way to live but rather that there is a vast range of lifestyles people subscribe to. Identity encompasses many variables and significantly impacts your value system and the way you conduct yourself daily. Being culturally sensitive means living your life the way you feel comfortable – but also accepting that other people choose to live differently without elevating your culture as superior. Supremacist ideas of ranking cultures have resulted in some of the worst atrocities on the planet. Therefore, the stakes are high when it comes to cultural sensitivity.

On a more micro scale, showing appreciation for what you admire in other cultures builds bridges that propel you into novel social environments. For example, you might tell a Mexican person you recently met how much you enjoy eating enchiladas, to which they may reply with an invite to a family gathering because, according to them, their aunt makes the best enchiladas in the world. Simple gestures that show you care are meaningful. What people hold dear to their hearts is often culturally influenced. For example, people who grew up in middle-class US homes in the 1980s probably have a connection with G.I Joe or Voltron toys. By showing appreciation for this cultural aspect of their earliest memories, you can lay the foundation for meaningfully bonding about something as trivial as their childhood toys.

Showing cross-cultural respect and appreciation will make it more likely that people will respect your way of life. There are probably culturally influenced beliefs and practices you subscribe to that you would find highly offensive if someone trampled on them. On the flip side of that coin, you would feel a comforting warmth if they expressed interest in learning about the particular aspects of your culture. Your openness to learn may encourage others to feel at ease enough to question you about how you grew up and the background you came from. Now, you'll be able to build on the shared ground of learning from one another based on your societal experiences. When you show respect to others, the same will come back around to you. Small talk that acknowledges diversity allows you to share what you hold as true and meaningful while opening your eyes to a completely new set of ideas that someone else may have.

Cultural Etiquette

The last thing you want to do when having small talk with someone or attempting to establish a connection is to insult them. Social cues, research, and asking questions can prevent you from making the cultural slip-ups that alienate people. Humans are not robots, so people know you are not from the same culture they subscribe to. Be open about your ignorance and allow yourself to be guided and informed. Arrogantly asserting yourself while diminishing the customs of others is the perfect way to make sure that you are hated. The rules of *your society* are not the rules of *all societies.* For example, in the Western world, it is common to put food on separate plates and eat with utensils like spoons or forks, while in some cultures in Africa and the Arab world, people eat from one plate using their hands. If you come into an environment where it is common to share food from one plate and you turn your nose up in disgust when they offer to share, do not expect that group to have any respect for you.

Social rules change according to area, culture, and setting. When you are in unfamiliar environments, mimicking is the safest bet for you to learn etiquette. Before you can walk the line of etiquette according to the culture you are amongst, you must be aware that there are differences between your norms and the accepted practices of others. Acknowledging that etiquette can shift between groups puts you in a great position to learn. Many of the daily activities that people embrace are heavily ritualistic. For example, when someone sneezes, you are expected to say, "Bless you." Overlooking these nuanced, sometimes minimal changes between cultures can land you in hot water if you are not humble enough to receive correction. What may seem weird to you is an everyday reality for many people. Remaining conscious that there are distinctions between what is considered polite amongst varying groups will keep you informed enough to adapt quickly.

When you specifically zoom in on small talk, etiquette can highlight which topics you should bring up in conversation. For some cultures, it is taboo to speak about religion or politics, and for others, it is a casual dinner chat. Paying attention to tone and body language will help you navigate the slippery minefield of cultural etiquette. If you notice resistance and discomfort, you can ask what you said that was inappropriate, or if you are not that comfortable asking, you can simply switch subjects. Be mindful of boundaries so that the way you engage in discussions is respectful, compassionate, and kind to varying backgrounds and upbringings.

An Open Heart and Mind to Expand Your Horizons

Although intellectually understanding diversity can be beneficial, there is nothing quite like an emotional connection to allow yourself to expand your horizons. Allowing yourself to get submerged into the culture of others will be impactful and memorable. For example, if you are attending a traditional event and notice that there is a particular dance that all the guests participate in, jump in the dance as well instead of being a spectator. Sharing in this joyful emotion will solidify any bonds that you have pursued. Opening your heart is all about allowing yourself to love what the people you are with love. Maybe some things are not for you, but you'll never know unless you try them out.

Many decisions that individuals make are not based on logic but are emotionally driven. Therefore, connecting with a culture on an emotional level will give you that unexplainable magnetism that is birthed from openness. There are some dishes that people know will not be well received outside of their group. Imagine coming into that environment as an outsider and being willing to try the strange dish. Even if you do not like it all that much, your willingness to try is enough to earn respect amongst the group. Approach intercultural exchange in a child-like manner. Children are willing to try more than adults and are easily convinced to go on new adventures. If you look at the world through child-like eyes where everything is novel, you can open your heart enough not only to engage with new people but also to fall in love with the way they do things.

The emotion that people have when it comes to their roots and identity is strong because this is what they learned at an early age from the people who care about them the most. The world's most intelligent scientist can tell you a piece of information, but if it contradicts what your grandmother taught, you'll probably reject it. The affinity one feels toward one's own traditions often does not come from logic, so you cannot reason your way into understanding it. Keeping an open heart and mind allows you to mirror the feelings that people you communicate with have for their cultural inheritance.

From Stereotypes to Understanding: Rethinking Assumptions Through Conversation

An amazing story of finding cultural overlaps in the most unlikely places is the journey of Daryl Davis. Davis is an African-American man who regularly attends Ku Klux Klan meetings. Davis has obtained the robes of over 200 Klan members whom he convinced to leave the racist organization. Davis began his conversion of Klan members in one of the most random places. After performing at a bar called the Silver Dollar Lounge, a man approached Davis, commenting how he had never heard a black man play piano like Jerry Lee Lewis. During their conversation, Davis explained to him that Lewis learned how to play piano in that uniquely skillful way from a blues tradition that predated him. The Klan member was not convinced, asserting that Jerry Lee Lewis had invented the sound.

Once the Klan member had revealed that he was a part of the racist organization, Davis did not allow himself to feel offended. Instead, he had a series of friendly conversations with the man. By relating to the racist man on a human level and not focusing on argumentative judgment, the Klan member eventually delivered his robes to Davis, celebrating that he had left the organization. Davis found the common ground of music to connect with the Klan members. By spending time with him and breaking the misconceptions that he held about black people, he was able to cut through the indoctrination of white supremacy that the Klan members had embraced.

With open and honest conversation where all parties listen to one another, Davis was able to reform countless of the most extreme racists.

Being willing to go into unfamiliar environments where the views of people are directly opposed to yours can produce miracles. No one would imagine that a black man could convince Ku Klux Klan members to drop their racist flags. With an open heart, Davis was able to break through the hardest shells to reveal the humanity that is hidden deep beneath trauma and misconceptions. Daryl Davis is literally the Ku Klux Klan's worst enemy as a black man, yet with an open mind and the tool of conversation, he managed to change the minds of many men who were convinced he was subhuman.

Chapter 6: Networking and Professional Small Talk

In the professional world, networking is like making new friends. It helps you grow, find opportunities, and succeed. Small talk is a part of networking, and it's more important than you might think. It's about having casual conversations with people you meet at work events or online. Doing this well can help you build strong relationships and open up new possibilities. This chapter explores networking and professional small talk, breaking down the techniques that turn simple chats into meaningful connections. You'll learn to start conversations, keep them interesting, and make networking work for you. It's all about making your professional journey better and more successful.

In the professional world, networking is like making new friends.

Significance of Workplace Networking

Building Bridges: Workplace networking is like building a web of connections within your professional environment. These connections create pathways to new opportunities. They can lead to collaboration on exciting projects, offer insights and learning from colleagues, or open doors to career advancement.

Knowledge Sharing: Networking at work is more than just knowing people; it's about tapping into the collective wisdom and experience of your peers. It's your access pass to the treasure trove of knowledge, best practices, and valuable information that can help you excel in your professional life.

Support and Collaboration: In a networked workplace, you're not alone. You have a built-in support system. Colleagues and superiors who know and trust you are more likely to lend a helping hand when you need it. Collaboration is smoother, and together, you can overcome challenges more effectively.

Career Advancement: Networking is often the stepping stone to career advancement. It can lead to promotions, new job opportunities, and professional growth. By building a positive reputation through your network, you're more likely to be considered for roles that fit with your career goals.

First Impressions Among Co-workers

Professionalism: Making a solid first impression in the workplace starts with professionalism. This means dressing appropriately for your role, being punctual, and respecting your work environment. Your behavior should mirror the collective culture and expectations of your workplace.

Positive Attitude: A positive attitude can be a game-changer. It involves being enthusiastic, friendly, and approachable. When your colleagues see you as someone who radiates positivity, it creates a more enjoyable work atmosphere and can enhance your professional reputation.

Active Listening: Listening is a critical component of first impressions. When you listen actively and show genuine interest in what your co-workers say, you're showing that you have respect for them, and you're making a lasting impression as someone who values and acknowledges others.

Respect and Courtesy: Being respectful and courteous towards your colleagues is fundamental. It means treating others with politeness, consideration, and empathy. By showing respect and courtesy in your interactions, you're building trust and a positive reputation in the workplace.

Timely Responses: When a co-worker reaches out to you, it's essential to respond in a timely manner. Prompt responses convey that you respect their time and value their communication. It sets a standard of respect in your professional relationships.

Meeting Commitments: If you make promises or commitments during your connections with your colleagues, it's crucial to follow through on them. Meeting your commitments shows reliability and trustworthiness, which are fundamental for building strong professional relationships.

Regular Updates: Keep your colleagues informed about developments or progress on shared projects. Regular updates ensure that everyone involved is on the same page. It reduces the likelihood of misunderstandings and paves the way for smooth collaboration.

Appreciation and Gratitude: Expressing appreciation and gratitude when your co-workers assist or collaborate with you is a powerful practice. A simple thank you goes a long way in building positive relationships. It shows that you acknowledge and value their contributions.

Cultivation of Mutually Beneficial Relationships

Give and Take: Mutually beneficial relationships thrive on reciprocity. It's not a one-sided gain but a two-way street. You should not only seek what you can gain but also consider what you can contribute. Offer your expertise, support, and assistance to your colleagues when they need it.

Mutually beneficial relationships thrive on reciprocity.
https://www.pexels.com/photo/man-and-woman-near-table-3184465/

Understanding Needs: To create mutually beneficial relationships, it's essential to understand the needs, challenges, and goals of your co-workers. When you know what's important to them, you can tailor your support to be more helpful and relevant.

Building Trust: Trust is the cornerstone of mutually beneficial relationships. Consistently demonstrating reliability, integrity, and ethical behavior is the way you build trust, and when your colleagues trust you, they're more likely to collaborate, share opportunities, and provide support.

Communication and Feedback: Open and honest communication is crucial. Give constructive feedback when needed, and be open to receiving it. Healthy dialogue promotes trust and understanding, leading to mutual growth and teamwork.

Making impactful first impressions, maintaining consistent follow-ups, and cultivating mutually beneficial relationships are vital to effective workplace networking. When executed thoughtfully and authentically, these practices can lead to a wealth of opportunities, support, and a fulfilling and successful career.

The Authentic Networking Philosophy

Authentic networking is grounded in the belief that relationships are the lifeblood of professional growth. It centers on a relationship-centric approach, emphasizing that your network should not be a collection of contacts but a circle of peers with whom you genuinely connect. Trust and reliability are fundamental. In authentic networking, commitments are not merely transactional; they represent your commitment to being dependable and trustworthy. This philosophy seeks mutual growth, emphasizing that networking is not a one-sided endeavor but a partnership where both parties actively contribute to each other's success and well-being.

Building Trust and Credibility

Building trust is a continuous process that relies on consistency and reliability. When you commit, it's more than just a promise; it underlines your reliability. Authentic relationships thrive on honesty and transparency. When you encounter challenges or need assistance, sharing your concerns with your network is a sign of trust. Furthermore, respect and courtesy are integral components. Treating your professional contacts with respect and courtesy reflects the value you place on their contributions to your journey as well as theirs.

Collaboration over Competition

Authentic networking prioritizes collective growth over individual competition. Knowledge and insights are freely shared within the network for everyone's benefit. If you discover a valuable resource or possess information, sharing it with your peers strengthens the connection. Providing support is another cornerstone of authentic networking. It's built on offering assistance, feedback, or mentorship when needed. While keeping the spirit of collaboration alive, don't forget to celebrate your success with your network and treat it as a shared accomplishment. This culture of celebration further strengthens the bonds within your network.

Nurturing Long-Term Relationships

Relationships built within authentic networks are not static. They evolve. Nurturing long-term relationships involves consistent communication. Regular check-ins, updates, and sharing of progress or challenges go toward keeping connections strong. As your career progresses, your networking needs change. In the authentic networking paradigm, you adapt to these changes by identifying new connections and nurturing existing ones as you grow. Lastly, legacy-building is a crucial aspect. In authentic networking, the focus is not solely on the present but also on the legacy you leave. Contributing positively to your network's growth and success is a testament to your commitment to authentic and enduring relationships.

Cultivating Meaningful Professional Relationships

In the intricate landscape of the professional world, the ability to cultivate and nurture meaningful relationships is a skill of paramount importance. Whether navigating a corporate setting, building a business, or advancing your career, the quality of your professional relationships can significantly impact your success, satisfaction, and growth. Here's how to cultivate meaningful professional relationships, dissecting the principles, strategies, and practices that build connections through trust, collaboration, and shared success.

Authenticity as the Foundation

Authenticity is the bedrock upon which meaningful professional relationships are built. Being authentic means being true to yourself and your values while interacting with others. It forms the basis of trust in your relationships, as people are more likely to connect with and confide in those who are genuine and transparent.

- Be honest about your strengths and weaknesses.
- Communicate openly.
- Show vulnerability when it's appropriate.
- Align your words and actions with your values.

Active Listening and Empathy

Active listening and empathy are twin pillars of meaningful professional relationships. Actively listening to others—fully engaging in the conversation, asking clarifying questions, and showing genuine interest—demonstrates your respect and attentiveness. Empathy, on the other hand, involves understanding and sharing the feelings of others. It's the ability to put yourself in their shoes and acknowledge their perspectives and emotions.

- Maintain eye contact and avoid distractions when someone is speaking.
- Practice reflective listening, summarizing what you've heard to ensure understanding.
- Validate others' feelings and emotions even if you don't share them.

- Show empathy by offering support and understanding during challenges.

Consistency and Reliability

Cultivating meaningful relationships requires consistency and reliability. If you want to be seen as someone who can be counted on, it's essential to follow through on your commitments and consistently show up when needed. It builds trust, which is a cornerstone of any enduring relationship.

- Meet deadlines and honor your promises.

- Be punctual and reliable in your professional engagements.

- If you can't meet a commitment, communicate it as early as possible and propose alternatives.

- Stay true to your word and be dependable.

Mutual Value Exchange

The most meaningful professional relationships are often characterized by mutual value exchange. It's a give-and-take dynamic where both parties benefit. Whether it's sharing knowledge, providing support, or offering resources, the willingness to contribute to one another's success is a hallmark of such relationships.

- Be proactive in offering assistance and support.

- Share your knowledge, insights, and resources willingly.

- Be open to feedback and be receptive to others' contributions.

- Collaborate on projects and initiatives that align with shared goals.

Networking and Expanding Your Circle

Cultivating meaningful relationships extends beyond your immediate colleagues or associates. Actively expanding your network broadens the opportunities for making even more meaningful connections. It involves reaching out to people in diverse professional circles, attending events, and utilizing digital platforms to connect with professionals who share your interests or goals.

- Attend industry events, conferences, and seminars.

- Leverage online platforms like LinkedIn to connect with like-minded professionals.

- Seek mentorship and guidance from experienced individuals in your field.

- Engage in volunteer or community activities to expand your network.

Conflict Resolution and Difficult Conversations

In the journey of cultivating meaningful professional relationships, conflicts or challenging conversations may inevitably arise. The ability to handle conflict with maturity and diplomacy can, if navigated with care, strengthen relationships rather than weaken them. Resolving conflict involves open communication, active listening, and seeking mutually agreeable solutions.

- Address conflicts directly and professionally, avoiding personal attacks.
- Listen to the other party's perspective and seek common ground.
- Collaborate on finding solutions that benefit both sides.
- Maintain a constructive and positive tone, even during difficult conversations.

Appreciation and Gratitude

Expressing appreciation and gratitude is a powerful way to nurture meaningful relationships. When you acknowledge the contributions of others and express gratitude for their support, it reinforces the positive connection, motivates your team, and strengthens bonds.

- Say "thank you" for the assistance and support you receive.
- Offer genuine compliments to recognize others' achievements.
- Celebrate shared successes and milestones together.
- Send occasional notes of appreciation or small gestures of gratitude.

By including these practices in your professional communications, you can develop and sustain connections characterized by trust, collaboration, and shared success, ultimately enriching your career and personal satisfaction.

Strategies for Memorable Interactions

Networking events offer a unique opportunity to expand your professional horizons, establish new connections, and leave a lasting impression on potential collaborators, mentors, or future colleagues. However, making these meetings memorable requires a thoughtful approach that goes beyond mere small talk. This section delves into effective strategies for navigating networking events and creating inspiring and unforgettable connections.

Set Clear Objectives

Before you attend a networking event, set clear objectives. What do you want to achieve? Whether it's finding a mentor, securing new clients, or exploring career opportunities, having a specific purpose in mind will guide your actions and make them more impactful.

Prepare Your Elevator Pitch

Provide a succinct and interesting elevator pitch that highlights your qualifications, experience, and career objectives. Make it succinct, memorable, and audience-appropriate. Your elevator pitch ought to spark attention and encourage more discussion.

Practice Effective Non-Verbal Communication

Your body language, facial expressions, and eye contact often say more than your words. Maintain good posture, offer a firm handshake, and use open and inviting body language. These non-verbal cues convey confidence and approachability.

Be a Connector

A memorable networker often acts as a connector. If you meet two people who could benefit from knowing each other, make the introduction. This generous act not only benefits the people you connect with but also establishes you as a valuable resource.

Tell Compelling Stories

People remember stories more than facts or statistics. Share anecdotes or stories that relate to your professional journey or illustrate your values and skills. Storytelling humanizes you and makes you more relatable.

Express Gratitude

After a networking event, send follow-up emails or notes expressing gratitude to those you met. Thank them for their time and express your interest in further discussions. This simple act sets the stage for continuing the relationship.

Be Mindful of Time Management

Make sure to respect others' time.

Respect others' time by being mindful of the duration of your interactions. If you sense that a conversation has reached a natural ending point, gracefully transition to another connection to maximize your networking opportunities.

Continuous Learning

Reflect on your networking experiences and continuously learn from them. Adapt your strategies based on what works best for you and the specific events you attend. Networking is a skill that improves with practice and feedback.

Present Yourself Professionally

First impressions are significant, and you only get one chance to be the most memorable person at the event. Dress appropriately for it, considering its formality and industry norms. A polished appearance conveys professionalism and shows that you take the event seriously.

Master the Art of Small Talk

While small talk may seem superficial, it's often the starting point for meaningful interactions. Brush up on your small talk skills, and practice open-ended questions that stimulate more profound conversations.

Share Your Expertise

If you possess specialized knowledge or insights, don't hesitate to share them. Providing valuable information during conversations positions you as a valuable resource and makes you memorable.

Keep an Open Mind

Approach networking events with an open mind. You never know where a valuable connection might emerge. Avoid preconceived notions, and be open to meeting a diverse range of people.

You can make your interactions remarkable by setting clear objectives, being an active listener, practicing authenticity, and using effective non-verbal communication. Ultimately, these strategies will help you expand your professional network and open doors to new opportunities.

The Follow-up: Ensuring Long-Term Connection and Collaboration

Networking events provide valuable opportunities to initiate relationships, but the real magic happens in the follow-up. It's in the follow-up where you transform initial connections into lasting, meaningful relationships that lead to collaboration, mentorship, or even future business ventures. This section explores the art of follow-up, sharing strategies, and practices that can help you grow your connections long after the networking event has ended.

Send a Personalized Thank-You Email

Send personalized thank-you emails to the people you meet.
https://www.pexels.com/photo/black-and-gray-digital-device-193003/

Within a day or two after the event, send a personalized thank-you email to the people you met. Express your gratitude for their time and the insightful conversation. Mention a specific detail from your conversation to show that you were actively engaged and paying attention.

Reference Shared Interests or Goals

In your follow-up, reference any shared interests, goals, or potential areas of collaboration that you discussed during the event. This not only shows them your commitment to the relationship but also that you're genuinely interested in exploring opportunities together.

Offer Value

Be proactive in offering value to your new connections. This could be in the form of resources, information, or introductions to others in your network who may benefit them. When you indicate your willingness to help, it reinforces your credibility and the potential for a mutually beneficial relationship.

Schedule a Follow-up Meeting or Call

Take the initiative to schedule a follow-up meeting or call to continue your conversation. This demonstrates your commitment to nurturing the relationship. It could be a coffee meeting, a video call, or a more formal business meeting, depending on the nature of your connection.

Engage on Social Media

Connect with your new contacts on social media platforms like LinkedIn, X, or relevant professional networks. Engage with their posts, share relevant content, and participate in discussions within their online communities. This keeps you on their radar and encourages ongoing interaction.

Attend Industry or Community Events Together

If there are industry-related events, seminars, or community activities that align with your mutual interests, consider attending them together. This can be an excellent way to deepen your connection, share experiences, and collaborate on projects or initiatives.

Send Periodic Updates

Stay in touch by sending periodic updates on your professional progress, projects, or milestones. This keeps your connections informed about your journey and opens the door for potential collaboration or support.

Share Resources and Insights

When you come across articles, books, or resources that might be relevant to your contacts, share them. This positions you as a valuable source of information and enhances the quality of your connection.

Seek Feedback

Occasionally, ask for feedback or comment on projects or challenges you're working on. Your contacts' input can be valuable, and it also establishes your willingness to collaborate and learn from them.

Celebrate Successes Together

When you or your connections achieve milestones or successes, celebrate them together. Acknowledge and congratulate them on their achievements. This positive reinforcement strengthens your bond and reinforces the culture of collaboration.

Maintain Open Communication

If you encounter challenges or obstacles in your professional journey, don't hesitate to communicate them openly with your network. Authenticity in your interactions, even when discussing challenges, builds trust and invites support.

While it will take some time to master the skills required for better networking, the earlier you start practicing, the quicker you'll get results. However, excessive workload, common household problems, or relationship issues can slow professional growth. In situations like these, consider resolving these underlying problems so you can start building connections in your professional life that can take you to new heights in your career with a clear and focused mind.

Chapter 7: Navigating Social Anxiety

Social anxiety is the fear of embarrassing yourself, not making a good impression, or performing poorly in social environments. The symptoms of social anxiety include excessive sweating, shivering, and an increased heart rate. Social anxiety is relatively common, with about 13% of people experiencing it. Being socially anxious impacts your well-being because it can prevent you from building the necessary relationships to reach your full potential. Social anxiety goes beyond a few butterflies in your stomach and can be paralyzing. The feeling of distress in social environments is often tied to other mental health issues like depression or dysthymia. To truly address social anxiety, a comprehensive view must be used to look at the condition from multiple angles.

Social anxiety can prevent you from connecting with others.
https://www.pexels.com/photo/businessman-man-person-people-7640766/

You cannot master the art of small talk, connecting, and leaving a great first impression when a debilitating fear of interacting holds you back. Therefore, finding ways to overcome social anxiety is foundational for getting you out of your shell to share your light with the world. There are numerous causes for developing social anxiety, like bullying, ridicule, abuse, and other forms of childhood trauma. These deeply rooted fears cannot be cured overnight. Working through social anxiety requires dedication and constant effort. By making a few key changes and implementing useful protocols, you can escape the self-destructive cycle of being held back by anxiety.

By first understanding social anxiety and how it manifests and then using scientifically supported coping mechanisms and therapeutic techniques to address it, you can cautiously step out of your cocoon and glow. Although daily challenges arise, you can equip yourself with the mental and emotional tools to swim through the rough seas of social anxiety. Your experiences are valid and should never be diminished, but you shouldn't allow your social anxiety to hold you back from experiencing the richness of social interactions.

The Prevalence of Social Anxiety in the Modern World

Society is becoming more isolated. Technology has given everyone access to instant information, entertainment, and communication. However, an unforeseen side effect of this dive into virtual reality is that many are losing their ability to effectively socialize, which is resulting in an increased prevalence of social anxiety. Research gathered in Kolkata revealed that the use of social media increased the likelihood for medical students to develop anxiety and depression. The instantaneous overwhelming volume of communication coming from different platforms coupled with a toxic online environment that encourages negativity and bullying has a physiological impact on many people. This stress reaction to online communication could result in the development of social anxiety, which significantly influences career achievement and mental health.

Furthermore, a culture of hyper-competitiveness fueled by media consumption patterns adds to the list of fears that hold individuals back from expressing themselves openly. This bombardment of aspirational imagery feeds insecurity as people compare themselves to the fairytale images presented on social media and find themselves wanting. The mind internalizes this perception, creating awkwardness and anxiety in social gatherings. The necessity to take steps to reduce social anxiety is rising as the pressure of the digital world takes its toll. Moreover, the motivation to interact outside of digital spaces is rapidly diminishing as technology companies master holding your attention for as long as possible. As much as it is daunting, exposing yourself to anxiety-inducing social scenarios is one of the ways used to break the fear of interacting.

Exposure therapy is a technique psychologists use that allows patients to face their fears in a controlled and safe environment. Although this should not be attempted without the assistance of a medical professional, certain principles from the intervention can be easily applied in your life. If social groups give you anxiety and talking to people enhances that discomfort, you can try joining a sports club. A physical team activity is a great way to gradually introduce yourself to social exchanges. Firstly, a team is a relatively small group you'll regularly meet up with so you can get used to them. Secondly, you already share a common interest, which should make conversation easier because you play the same sport.

Thirdly, communication on the field is minimal and simple because you are focused on playing the game, so there is reduced pressure to be social. Lastly, you exert a lot of physical energy, which can distract you from negative feelings.

Your proactivity will determine your success, especially considering that society is being shaped in a way that adds to social anxiety. Anxiety can be the brick wall you run into when attempting to establish relationships or just generally be more open to conversation. If communicating better is your goal, this is the first hurdle to overcome because it is internal. Before you can think about improving relationships with others and being more sociable, you must first have a cordial relationship with yourself, which means the thoughts that fuel social anxiety must actively be transmuted for a positive outcome.

The Stigma of Social Anxiety

Although many people experience social anxiety, it is not often discussed because a stigma exists around being insecure and lacking confidence. Society values certain traits because human evolutionary development props up behaviors that benefit the group. One of the traits people value is trust. For individuals to trust you, it is important to appear sure of yourself. The discomfort and physiological symptoms of social anxiety are visible in behavior that communicates to people that you are unsure of yourself. This breaks people's confidence in you because you lack self-esteem.

Social anxiety often gets undermined by people who do not experience it, so they provide unhelpful advice, like telling you to simply get over yourself. Furthermore, the awkward behavior that is tied to social anxiety often results in bullying and alienation. Spreading awareness about social anxiety could help breed a more tolerant societal atmosphere down the line. It seems like society is moving in a positive direction because mental health is a topic that is prominent in the wider discourse. However, there is still a long way to go before social stigmas are broken around.

Wider education campaigns centering on social anxiety need to be established because of how uninformed the public is about it. Mismanaging social anxiety exponentially worsens its impact on your well-being because it can destroy the essential social skills you need to live a fulfilled life. In the worst case scenarios, self-harm or suicidal ideation could be induced by the isolation social anxiety disorder causes. Often, people will find themselves around individuals who do not understand how powerful the feelings of anxiety can be. This lack of knowledge means that a person's support system can fall short and not provide the help that is needed. Educating yourself about social anxiety allows you to communicate your needs clearly and explicitly and ask for the assistance you need from those close to you. From an informed position, you can make better choices to create the most conducive environment for you to excel socially.

The stigma surrounding social anxiety may also be a barrier preventing people from seeking out care. If your loved ones play down the seriousness of your social anxiety, especially in severe cases, it can be destructive. Therapeutic interventions led by a medical professional are necessary in some cases and can be useful for many. Neglecting the crucial treatment for social anxiety could have spillover effects that derail a multitude of sectors in your life. Through communication and education, you can reduce the stigma and implement the changes that you need to function optimally in social situations. Focusing on small talk before social anxieties are addressed can render the activity meaningless because you can't speak to someone you do not approach.

The Causes of Social Anxiety and How It Manifests

Social anxiety exists on a spectrum because most people experience some nervousness in unfamiliar situations. However, once your social anxiety reaches a certain threshold, its negative impacts become more apparent. People who have high levels of anxiety in social environments may have social anxiety disorder. The causes of the disorder are difficult to pin down because it is typically a complex mix of reasons for its development.

There may be genetic and neurological causes for social anxiety disorder. If you have family members who have the disorder and you experience the same symptoms, it may be a genetically inherited trait. It also may be because of an overactive amygdala, which is the fear center of the brain. Social anxiety disorder can be classified as a type of phobia, so the amygdala may play a significant role. The disorder usually develops between the ages of 11 and 19. Often, shy children evolve into adults with social anxiety disorder. The disorder developing during childhood has led many to believe that it may have something to do with upbringing and environment. Controlling and overbearing parents have higher instances of children with social anxiety because of the pressure to meet their unrealistic expectations. Abuse, bullying, and teasing also contribute to anxiety in social situations due to the fear of being ridiculed or harmed by a rejecting audience. Health conditions and physical appearances that draw negative attention could also facilitate the development of social anxiety disorder.

Depending on the context and setting, this disorder manifests in different ways. There are psychological, social, and physical ways that social anxiety shows up. Self-consciousness causes you to feel excessive fear when confronted with social environments. This fear can create a stress response that causes immense psychological strain. You'll find yourself worrying before, during, and after a social event, repeatedly analyzing every little action you took and the responses you got. This overthinking can result in you shrinking into the back of a crowd, hoping not to get noticed.

The emotional strain from the anxiety and stress presents itself physically with numerous symptoms. Your physical health and mental wellness are closely linked, majorly influencing one another. Your muscles will tense up, and you may begin to tremble. You also might feel dizzy and nauseous, which will only increase the discomfort you are feeling. The physical and psychological unease resulting from social anxiety encourages isolation. Sufferers will avoid eating in public or going shopping. They will be frightened of asking questions and may go as far as avoiding important meetings like job interviews. The combination of the mental, physical, and social outcomes of social anxiety can make it difficult for someone to maintain a healthy lifestyle.

Challenges of Social Anxiety in Daily Interactions

Isolating yourself due to social anxiety will stagnate your social skills. Interaction takes practice, so without making an effort to connect with people, your daily exchanges may be unmemorable and bland. People do not necessarily remember what you told them. It's more about how you made them feel. The symptoms of social anxiety might cause people to feel uncomfortable around you, or it could keep you from truly engaging in conversation, making you easily forgettable.

Overcoming low self-esteem and self-consciousness is a daily challenge for people who have severe social anxiety. Interactions that seem natural and fluid for others require sufferers to dig deep and use all their energy for this simple exchange. Like someone with asthma needs an inhaler to participate in sports, a person with crippling social anxiety would need the support of therapeutic interventions for average, routine social exchanges. Therefore, not knowing about the disorder could have someone stumbling around in the dark and developing unhealthy coping mechanisms like substance abuse. Self-medicating anxiety can be the root of many addictions.

Talking to a stranger may be second nature to many, but menial tasks like ordering a pizza over the phone or chatting with the cashier while you wait for your change could morph into something nightmarish. The extra mental load of constantly thinking about everyday social interactions, both past and present, is draining. Social interactions become a complicated maze or a tangled web of misunderstanding and worry. Natural concerns about people become a point of hyper-fixation that prevents you from establishing relationships because you fear being embarrassed or rejected. Making friends becomes difficult, and networking for economic opportunities is an impossible mission.

To avoid the churning internal turmoil when you are in social environments, you may be driven to isolate. People with social anxiety spend a lot of time alone daily, but this is a temporary relief and does not address the root of the problem. Hiding from the world is just you hiding from your thoughts and feelings. Loneliness and isolation contribute to developing depression because strong social bonds are essential to maintaining mental health. Social anxiety that goes unaddressed can quickly devolve into a nightmarish self-fulfilling prophecy that affirms the negative self-talk. Proactively combating social anxiety is the only way forward if you aim to live a well-rounded life.

Managing Your Social Anxieties with Therapeutic Interventions and Coping Mechanisms

The impacts of social anxiety can be dire, but this does not mean all hope is lost. Embracing healthy coping mechanisms and practicing professionally endorsed therapeutic interventions like cognitive behavioral therapy, acceptance and commitment therapy, exposure therapy, and group sessions could uplift you to the heights of a social butterfly. Each of these methods has its own benefits, so you'll need to find what best works for you. Consulting a professional is the best course of action to take, but if that is not possible, some simple exercises can help you gain the confidence to excel in conversation and navigate a social environment smoothly.

Cognitive behavioral therapy, or **CBT**, is one of the primary means used to treat social anxiety. CBT is a method of addressing negative thought patterns by working through them to discover your triggers and what actions you can take to shift your thoughts and promote more positive behavior. Journaling is a key practice of CBT. Daily journaling lets you process the events of the day and your thoughts to pinpoint moments where you could have adjusted your behavior, as well as allowing you to introspect. CBT is great for unpacking the root causes of your social anxiety and drafting individualized plans to improve your social skills.

Another therapeutic approach that is often used successfully is acceptance and commitment therapy or **ACT**. The basis of ACT is to encourage patients to fully accept their emotions and thoughts but also realize that they may be mismatched responses to adverse situations. You cannot change unwanted responses by being in denial or invalidating how you feel. Every thought and emotion has a reason for coming forward. Once you identify the emotions and their triggers, you can take conscious action to change your responses to distressing situations. Both ACT and CBT use some mindfulness practices. Mindfulness is about becoming aware of yourself within the moment. The next time you find yourself feeling anxious, take a few deep breaths and focus on your breathing. Repeat the mantra "I am whole. I am worthy. I am here to contribute. And I will be received well." Breathing and chanting at the moment can break you out of self-destructive cycles. Excusing yourself for a moment to gather your thoughts could do wonders.

Group therapy is a great way to connect with people experiencing similar issues. Finding a group to discuss your experiences with it kills two birds with one stone because you are getting practice socializing while getting the opportunity to delve into your experiences with anxiety with people who understand. Discussing your problems brings awareness to the fact that you are not alone. You can take the initiative to form a support group. You can start online and gradually work your way to real-life meet-ups. Being proactive in finding community will accelerate your progress to enhance your social skills.

Accounts of Social Anxiety

Sara experienced success addressing her social phobia with a combination of CBT and exposure therapy. Sara is a 37-year-old female who suffers from OCD in addition to her social anxiety. Due to her OCD and anxiety, Sara developed a fear of blushing in public. After a few sessions of slowly getting exposed to groups of people in a safe environment with the reassurance of a counselor, Sara was able to make long-term improvements and exponentially improve her social skills. Sara's treatment included talk therapy, mindfulness exercises, and journaling. She has kept applying many of the techniques she learned and says that she is constantly improving and learning new things. She has been able to attend a number of social events and has managed to make new acquaintances along the way.

Mike's story can be used as an example of how social phobia is diagnosed. When Mike was first diagnosed, he was a little younger than Sara: twenty years old. He described and explained how he was bullied throughout his schooling by people calling him dumb and a loser. When Mike gets nervous, he tends to stutter, sweat, and feel uncomfortable in his skin. Mike went on to explain that his schoolwork suffered. After all, he always felt intimidated to raise his hand and ask a question because he thought it would reinforce the comments people made about him being dumb. He became avoidant, often ignoring his phone and skipping class so as not to have to deal with the discomfort of the adverse social environment. Furthermore, he often found himself looping conversations in his mind, zooming in on the smallest details.

With this example, it is clear how Mike's social anxiety negatively affected his life. The physiological impacts, like stuttering, resulted in him getting teased, which just stoked the flames of his disorder. Furthermore, his avoidance behavior, like ignoring calls, prevented him from making friends, while his shyness in class affected his academic progress. With some coping mechanisms, like taking a few deep breaths before speaking or questioning the assumptions he made when replaying conversations, Mike could make progress toward overcoming social anxiety.

Chapter 8: The Art of Body Language

Talking isn't the only way you share what's going on inside your head and heart. You also communicate with your body, and this hidden language is called "body language." Think of it like a secret code that tells others how you feel and what you mean without using words. This body language is familiar; your ancestors used it before they even had fancy words. It's hardwired into you. Even today, it's just as important as talking when expressing emotions and thoughts.

In this journey through body language, you'll learn about all the little signs your body gives off, like hand movements, how you stand, the expressions on your face, and how your eyes move. Understanding body language helps you connect with people better, figure out what they're thinking and feeling, and handle all sorts of situations, whether talking with friends, working with colleagues, or making deals.

Gestures

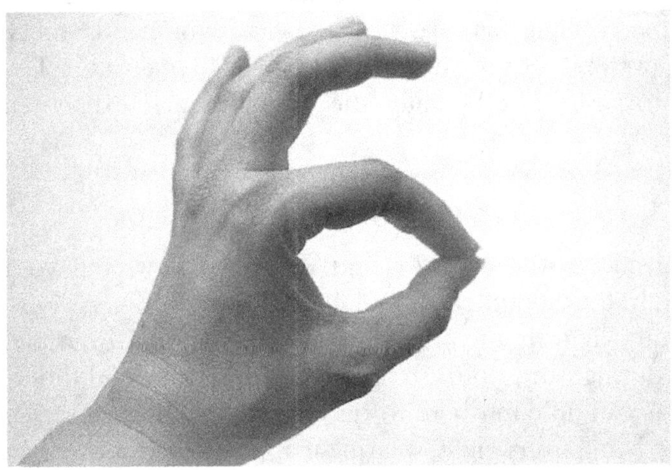

Gestures can complement your words.

Gestures can be a powerful way to emphasize or complement your words. For instance, when you express excitement, your hands may naturally gesture upward or your body lean forward, reinforcing your verbal message. These gestures make your emotional state more evident and resonate with others.

Contradicting Verbal Messages

On the flip side, gestures can also contradict your verbal communication. If you say "I'm fine" while clenching your fists or crossing your arms, your gestures may convey tension or discomfort, indicating that you may not be okay after all.

Cultural Variations

It's essential to be aware that gestures don't always have the same interpretations in every culture. A friendly or neutral gesture in one culture could be perceived differently in another. Awareness of these nuances can help you avoid misunderstandings and connect effectively with people from diverse backgrounds. For example, the peace sign is recognized globally as a symbol of peace and goodwill.

However, some innocuous gestures in one culture could be offensive in another. It's crucial to be aware of these cultural differences to prevent misunderstandings. Research shows that gestures amplify the emotional content of speech. They engage the motor cortex and the emotional centers of the brain, reinforcing the spoken message.

Suppose you're sharing an exciting story with a friend. As you describe the thrilling part, you may notice your hands subconsciously gesturing widely, conveying the moment's intensity. This natural tendency to gesture accentuates the emotions and excitement in your storytelling.

Postures

It's the position of your body and describes how well your spine is aligned with the shoulders, head, and lower body. A lousy posture develops quickly without you even recognizing it. For example, reclining in a chair during work hours, carrying heavy objects, and doing repetitive movements can all contribute to developing a bad posture. Some other factors like being overweight, wearing inappropriate footwear, or having a condition like scoliosis can also affect your posture.

Open vs. Closed Postures

Your posture and body language can speak volumes about your confidence and receptiveness. An open posture, characterized by an upright, relaxed stance, can convey confidence and a welcoming attitude. In contrast, a closed posture with crossed arms and hunched shoulders can indicate defensiveness or discomfort.

Power Poses

Some postures, often called power poses, are believed to boost confidence and assertiveness. These include standing tall with your hands on your hips or leaning back in a chair. While their effectiveness is debated, they underline the role of body language in shaping your self-perception and communication. There are several other power poses you can use to emphasize points while conversing, but most of them can be used in informal situations. Therefore, stick with the power poses you think will sync well with your personality and communication style.

Adaptation to Situational Context

Your postures can be adapted to different situational contexts. For example, in a formal meeting, sitting up straight with good posture conveys professionalism, while slouching may suggest disinterest or fatigue. Adapting your posture to match the situation improves your ability to communicate effectively. You may be surprised to know, but body postures impact hormone levels. An open, expansive posture can increase testosterone (linked to confidence) and decrease cortisol (related to stress), influencing how you feel and others perceive you.

Consider a job interview. When you sit up straight, maintain eye contact, and have an open posture, you not only feel more confident but also project this confidence to the interviewer, potentially improving your chances of success.

Facial Expressions

Micro Expressions

Your face can involuntarily reveal your genuine emotions through micro-expressions—fleeting, subtle expressions that last only a fraction of a second. These microexpressions often betray your genuine feelings, even when you're trying to conceal them. Understanding and interpreting these microexpressions can give you a great deal of information about the emotions of others. Microexpressions are involuntary and often reveal genuine emotions. They occur due to rapid muscle contractions in the face, reflecting underlying feelings even when someone is trying to conceal them.

Imagine a colleague who says they're okay with a new project but quickly flashes a microexpression of anxiety. You catch this fleeting cue, prompting you to ask if they have any concerns, ultimately leading to a more open and honest discussion.

Smiles

A smile is one of the most universally recognized facial expressions.
https://www.pexels.com/photo/two-yellow-emoji-on-yellow-case-207983/

A smile is one of the most universally recognized and positive facial expressions. It communicates friendliness, warmth, and approachability. Likewise, a genuine smile involving your mouth and eyes is compelling in building rapport and trust. People will be comfortable sharing their feelings when they perceive your smile as a gesture of understanding and empathy, easing any stress or conflict lingering in the air. These reduced tensions promote collaboration, problem-solving, and conflict resolution, creating a harmonious environment where teamwork thrives.

Emotion Recognition

As you work on your gestures, posture, and expressions, focus on the body language others portray. Improving your ability to recognize and interpret facial expressions is a fundamental aspect of human interaction. Understanding the nuances of facial expressions helps you to gauge the emotions and intentions of others accurately. Developing this skill can intensify empathy and help you navigate social interactions more effectively.

While gestures and postures are portrayed differently throughout cultures, facial expressions are universal to humans. Studies have shown that people from different cultures can accurately identify emotions like happiness, anger, and sadness based on facial cues. Think about when you greeted a friend with a warm, genuine smile. The immediate connection and positive energy generated by this simple facial expression demonstrate the universal language of smiles.

Eye Movements

Eye contact influences oxytocin release, often called the bonding hormone. Oxytocin is associated with trust and social connection, and it's released when you establish eye contact with others. You may have had a meaningful conversation with a loved one. When you look deeply into their eyes while discussing something heartfelt, you are not only connecting on an emotional level but also releasing oxytocin, strengthening your bond.

Making Eye Contact

Although sustained eye contact signifies attentiveness, confidence, and engagement, excessive or overly intense eye contact can be perceived as aggressive or invasive. Striking the right balance between *how long* and *too long* your eye contact is crucial for effective communication.

Avoidance and Shifting

Avoiding eye contact or frequently shifting your gaze signals discomfort, anxiety, or deceit. It suggests you're not fully present in the conversation or might be concealing something. Recognizing these cues in yourself and others can help you navigate social dynamics more effectively.

Pupil Dilation

Pupil dilation is mostly an involuntary response to various emotions, including interest, environmental changes, attraction, or stress. Dilated pupils can reveal your emotional state, sometimes more reliably than your words. Understanding the significance of pupil dilation in yourself and others can give you invaluable information. A relatable example of pupil dilation can be your first date. As you connect with your date and the conversation becomes more engaging, you notice their pupils dilating, revealing their genuine interest and attraction to you into emotional reactions and intentions.

Body language, including gestures, postures, facial expressions, and eye movements, is a rich and intricate form of communication that often amplifies or contradicts your verbal messages. Mastering the art of body language involves self-awareness of your non-verbal cues and a keen ability to interpret and respond to the cues of those around you. This chapter provides valuable insights into the non-verbal language that underlies your daily interactions and offers practical tools for improving your communication skills.

The Silent Vocabulary of Hands and Posture

Although hand gestures and postures are explained briefly, here's how the silent vocabulary of gestures and postures can make communication more expressive.

Complementing Verbal Communication

Hand gestures often add a tremendous amount to your verbal communication. They help emphasize and clarify spoken words, making the message more vivid and engaging. For instance, when you say the mountain was *so high* (and use your hands to indicate height), you not only provide a visual image but also intensify the impact of your words.

Revealing Emotions

Your hand movements can reveal your emotions. When you're excited, your hands may gesture upward, mirroring your exhilaration. This non-verbal cue adds depth and authenticity to your expression.

Interpersonal Connection

Body language and hand gestures play a crucial role in establishing rapport with others. More effectively than words, a warm embrace, a comforting slap on the back, or just holding hands can express love, support, and comfort. You may throw your arms up in the air and leap, expressing your happiness in a way that is beyond words.

Honesty and Deception

On the flip side, non-verbal cues often reveal deception. When someone's gestures and postures don't align with their spoken words, it can be a sign of dishonesty. Fidgeting, such as tapping one's fingers or shifting restlessly, can betray nervousness or the intent to conceal the truth.

Enhanced Listening

Proficiency in decoding non-verbal cues elevates your listening skills. While someone speaks, their gestures and postures indicate where their emotions are at, allowing you to understand their perspective and respond empathetically. For example, if someone talks about a challenging experience while hunched over with a furrowed brow, it indicates their discomfort and distress, even if they don't explicitly say so.

Understanding the silent language of hand gestures and posture is a journey into the complex world of non-verbal communication. Mastering this language gives you a deeper appreciation of the thoughts and emotions of those around you. It allows you to connect more profoundly, foster meaningful relationships, and navigate social interactions with heightened awareness and sensitivity.

The Power of Eye Contact

Eye contact is not just a simple act of looking into another person's eyes; it's a fundamental component of human communication that profoundly impacts our interpersonal interactions. The ability to establish and maintain eye contact is a skill that transcends spoken language and plays a pivotal role in how people connect, engage, and convey their thoughts and emotions to others. Here's why eye contact is crucial and its influence on several life aspects.

Establishing Connection

The gaze you share with someone creates an immediate connection. When you make eye contact, it signifies you are fully present and engaged in the conversation, forging a bridge of understanding between you and the other person.

Signaling Attentiveness

Eye contact serves as a clear signal that you are actively listening and paying close attention to the speaker. It assures them that their words are not falling on deaf ears but are being heard and valued, nurturing an environment of open and honest communication.

Building Trust

Trust, a cornerstone of effective communication, is often cultivated through eye contact. Maintaining eye contact can communicate sincerity, transparency, and authenticity. This, in turn, fosters trust and a sense of mutual understanding, which is integral to healthy relationships.

Emotional Expression

The eyes are an eloquent tool for expressing emotions. They convey happiness, sadness, anger, or empathy, allowing the other person to understand your emotional state and your feelings.

Conveying Confidence

The ability to hold solid and appropriate eye contact is closely associated with confidence. It signifies that you are self-assured and comfortable in a given situation. This confidence can positively influence how others perceive your competence and authority.

Respect and Courtesy

In many cultures, making eye contact is a gesture of respect and courtesy. It signifies that you acknowledge the other person as an equal and are genuinely interested in what they say, enhancing the quality of your interactions. On the contrary, there are Eastern cultures that encourage avoiding eye contact with the elderly and consider eye gaze as a gesture of disrespect during conversations. Nonetheless, it's better to know about the cultural norms of the region you live in to avoid such instances.

Eye Contact During Communication

Active Listening

Eye contact is an essential component of active listening. It not only encourages the speaker to continue sharing their thoughts and emotions but also signals your unwavering attention and support for their expression. On the contrary, not making adequate eye contact while listening shows you are not attentively listening or showing interest.

Empathy and Connection

When you maintain eye contact, you hear the speaker's words and connect with their emotions. This deepens your understanding of their perspective and equips you to respond with empathy and support, strengthening your bond.

Reducing Misunderstandings

By making eye contact, you position yourself to catch subtle non-verbal cues from the speaker, including tone or body language changes. This heightened awareness can reduce misunderstandings and facilitate more effective communication.

Social and Professional Benefits

Networking and Social Skills

As explained earlier, proficient eye contact in social settings and networking opportunities can leave a positive impression and enable you to forge meaningful connections with others.

Professional Success

In your professional life, eye contact is closely linked to confidence and competence. It can have a positive impact on job interviews, negotiations, and leadership roles, contributing to your overall success.

Conflict Resolution

When engaging in challenging conversations or conflict resolution, eye contact can create a more open and honest exchange, making it easier to address issues and find common ground.

Eye contact is a fundamental aspect of human communication that extends far beyond mere visual interaction. It serves as a universal signal of connection, attentiveness, and trust, which can profoundly impact your relationships, both in personal and professional spheres. Understanding the importance of eye contact and refining your ability to use it in your interactions can significantly contribute to building more robust, authentic, and empathetic connections with others. It is a silent yet potent means of conveying respect, empathy, and authenticity in the complex landscape of human communication.

Aligning Verbal and Non-Verbal Communication

Alignment between your verbal and non-verbal communication is essential for delivering messages that are both clear and consistent. When your words and non-verbal cues are harmonious, your audience can grasp your intended message more easily. You might have seen motivational speakers delivering life-changing lectures. They all work heavily on the harmony between their non-verbal and verbal communication methods, which lets them connect with their audience and convey an impactful message. Imagine yourself delivering a pitch to industry conglomerates. If your communication game is up to the mark, investors will listen to you attentively, engage further, and increase your credibility.

Enhancing Credibility

Inconsistencies between what you say and how you say it can destroy your credibility. People tend to trust individuals whose verbal and non-verbal communication match, as it signals authenticity and honesty.

Facilitating Understanding

Just because you command a topic doesn't mean the people you engage with have the same knowledge as you. Before delivering your message, it's better to think about how your message will be understood or perceived by others. An aligned message is inherently more straightforward to understand. It delivers a holistic experience of your communication, making it more comprehensive and accessible to your audience. Don't be afraid to play with words and tweak your conversations accordingly.

Elements of Alignment

Body Language

Your body language, including your posture, gestures, and facial expressions, plays a significant role in alignment. When you convey excitement about a topic, your body language should mirror this enthusiasm with lively gestures and an upright posture.

Tone of Voice

Your tone, pitch, and the cadence of your voice are equally important. The tone of your voice can drastically alter the interpretation of your message. When discussing a sensitive matter, a calm and soothing tone reinforces a comforting message. Besides working on these factors, speak steadily and practice articulation for an impactful speech delivery.

Achieving Alignment

Self-Awareness

The cornerstone of aligning verbal and non-verbal communication is self-awareness. It requires a thorough understanding of your non-verbal habits and how they might differ from your verbal communication. Recognize any discrepancies and actively work to bring them into harmony. You can start by noting your facial expressions, body posture, tone of voice, and eye contact while having random conversations at work to know how you react. It will take some time and patience to develop a higher sense of self-awareness, but the output you'll get can prove to be a revolutionary life skill in your arsenal.

Observation of Others

Effective communication goes both ways. To ensure alignment, you must convey and interpret messages accurately. Pay close attention to the non-verbal cues of others, as this helps you adjust your communication style to align with their expectations and needs more effectively. Observing how others communicate with you matters because it's somewhat useless if the other person is not showing interest or is at the same engagement level as you.

Ask the Right Questions

Instead of asking questions that can be answered with a yes or no, ask open-ended or opinion-based questions when trying to communicate. Asking a simple question can stall any conversation, while a rhetorical question sparks interest, making conversations fruitful. During conversations, you can also paraphrase in specific terms or generally to show what you understood. These practices act as an opportunity to harmonize your non-verbal and verbal communication skills.

Practice and Feedback

Achieving alignment will need practice. Seek feedback from people you trust, who can tell you how effectively you convey messages. Regular practice enables you to refine your alignment and improve your overall communication.

Adaptation

When engaging with individuals from diverse cultural backgrounds, adapt your non-verbal communication to match their expectations. This adaptability ensures your messages are well-received, culturally respectful, and clearly understood.

Aligning verbal and non-verbal communication is a complex process that demands self-awareness, observation, practice, and cultural sensitivity. It is not merely about matching your words with your non-verbal cues but also about delivering a holistic, trustworthy, and empathetic message. This alignment is the key to building effective relationships, fostering understanding, and conveying authenticity in your communication.

Chapter 9: Easing into Dialogue (When It Terrifies You)

Small talk may be a small step toward making a social impact, but it is a giant leap toward making meaningful conversations. If you have already practiced having small talk with people, you may have grown a little comfortable around them, but at the same time, you may be worried about what comes next. What happens after you make small talk?

Small talk can lead to meaningful conversations.

It's a nightmare situation for many people, especially because they don't know what's going to happen next. Small talk is a solid, dependable social crutch, but making meaningful conversation is like taking off the training wheels for the first time. You move forward into an unknown conversational realm, all the while struggling to keep your social balance. How do you keep the conversation going and steer it into more meaningful waters? How can you ease into dialogue, especially when it terrifies you?

Tackling the Fear

Small talk would have already reduced your fear of conversation. So, it's not exactly talking to someone that you are worried about. What you'll talk about – that is what probably terrifies you. What if you pick a topic and start speaking about it, and they don't like it? What if they get bored, drop the conversation midway, and just leave? It's this fear of what could happen that you need to get over. Here are a few tips that will help you tackle that fear.

• Focus on Your Breathing

Anxiety is putting those negative thoughts in your head. Often, the best way to overcome anxiety is to just breathe. As soon as your small talk ends and the fear of further dialogue creeps up on you, stop the conversation and excuse yourself. Focus on breathing in and out, and assure yourself that everything is going to go well.

• Embrace Positivity

Whenever the terror of failing at a conversation grips you and the first signs of negative thoughts haunt your mind, try to convert them into positive feelings. Think of positive affirmations like, "Nothing will go wrong if you take the conversation further." Embrace positivity and success instead of worrying about failure.

• Talk to a Friend

With a friend, a parent, or anyone else who is close to you, you don't need to think twice before making conversation. Try talking to a friend you haven't met for a long while. Engage in small talk before steering the conversation into reminiscing about the past. It's easy to make dialogue with a long-lost friend or acquaintance, and it will prepare you for making meaningful conversations with strangers.

Looking for Cues

You don't want to rush into a meaningful conversation after making small talk. It may be meaningful for you, but how do you know the other person won't find it boring? Even if they are interested in the topic, they may not want to get into a deep discussion just yet. Look for cues that signify their state of mind and level of interest in taking the conversation further.

• Verbal Cues

Verbal cues are clear verbal indications that show they want to dive deeper into the topic of the conversation.

> o Showing interest with full sentences like, "Hey, I didn't know that!" or, "That sounds like fun!"
>
> o Stressing their interest with adverbs like, "That's an absurdly confusing question," or, "It looks really interesting."
>
> o Genuinely empathizing, like, "I understand how you must be feeling," or, "That looks like a challenging prospect."
>
> o Asking questions that further the conversation, like, "How did they react to it?" or, "What happened next?"
>
> o Voicing their thoughts aloud, like, "Oh, so that's how it came about," or, "I was wondering how it went from there."

It is easy to understand and act on verbal cues because they will make you feel like moving ahead with the topic. On the other hand, if they are responding in monosyllables or saying something only after you have asked a question, it may indicate they want to end the conversation.

• Non-Verbal Cues

These may be slightly more difficult to catch, especially if you are interacting with a reserved person. Non-verbal cues are any facial expressions or body behavior that indicates their interest in the conversation.

> o Nodding at your affirmations

- o Eyes lighting up when you talk about a topic of interest
- o Having open body language, like standing with their arms to their sides or sitting with their palms on their thighs
- o Mirroring your body language, like shaking their head when you shake yours

Non-verbal cues like having dead eyes throughout the conversation, smiling without letting it reach their eyes, showing their side profile while talking, and rarely nodding as you speak are clear indications of disinterest in taking the conversation further.

- **Intuition**

If you are unable to recognize both verbal and non-verbal cues, or if the person you're speaking to doesn't normally react much during any conversation, your intuition will be your best bet. Intuition is your gut feeling, your instinct that tells you to keep going deeper into the conversation. There's no scientific or logical basis for this feeling. It's just a hunch.

Have your hunches been right more often than not? Are your instincts screaming that the person is indeed interested? Take a leap of faith and continue with the topic. If you are wrong, they will start showing negative cues soon after. Then, stop the conversation or move on to something else.

If they are displaying cues that show their disinterest, don't push it. Let the conversation end on a neutral note. At your next meeting, try to broach another topic they might be interested in. What if they start showing favorable cues?

Acting on Positive Cues

During your small talk, did your audience display any positive cues, verbal or non-verbal? It's time to show your interest, too, with your own positive cues. However, if you try to display all the cues mentioned above arbitrarily, it may seem like you are feigning interest. Here are a few ways to bring up those cues organically without really thinking about them.

• Active Listening

Active listening is a three-step process.

1. Hearing.
2. Understanding.
3. Showing that you understood.

You have to absorb what is being said and show that you are listening to them. Nod whenever a statement calls for it. Shake your head if they are saying something extraordinary. Punctuate your conversation with a healthy mix of "Hmm," "I see," "You don't say," "Okay," "I know," "That can't be," etc. These may be monosyllables, but they don't convey disinterest. They show the other person that you are listening to them.

• Interrupt Only When Absolutely Necessary

Constant interruptions convey to the talker that you are not really trying to listen to them but are simply making your own points. It is recommended not to interrupt at all. If you have doubts or wish to contribute something to their story, make a mental note of them and say them out loud only after they have finished talking. Can't understand the rest of the conversation without clearing a doubt first? Politely excuse yourself, apologize for the interruption, and then ask. If they have taken a long pause, contribute to the conversation after asking, "May I say something?"

• Ask Questions

This is for when they have finished talking or if they have taken a long pause. Ask questions about something you didn't understand. If you understood everything, just ask them if you understood it correctly. It shows that you are interested in what they have to say and want to take the conversation forward.

• Empathize

Warmly assuring you understand their situation and can relate to it opens many doors for additional dialogue. But what if you have never experienced what they are going through? Acknowledge that fact, and at the same time, say that you are sorry about their plight. Showing empathy is one of the very few things that can clear the way for a substantial conversation.

Effective Strategies for a Smooth Transition

Now that you know they are interested in making further conversation and you have also shown your interest, you should transition to that meaningful part of your interaction. Don't make an awkward transition, however. It may just prompt them to end the conversation.

Imagine that you just finished the small talk after discussing the weather. Out of the blue, they start talking about a rock concert they went to. It doesn't matter whether or not you like to listen to rock music. The break in your chain of thought from the weather to something entirely different will make you feel out of place in the conversation. Needless to say, you'll try to excuse yourself and leave.

Make a smooth transition from small talk to interesting, in-depth discussion. Your instincts will usually tell you the right time for the evolution in your interaction, but if they are not refined enough, follow these effective tips and strategies to get you started.

• Find Something to Talk About

This is the most basic step toward making any type of conversation. To bring meaning to your small talk, it becomes doubly important. You need to find common ground to make additional conversation. Don't hesitate to ask simple questions. They are expected, and it shows that you are willing to add more layers to the conversation.

> o What are your likes and dislikes?
>
> o What are your hobbies?
>
> o What kind of music do you listen to?
>
> o What kind of movies do you watch?
>
> o What do you do for a living?

Once you find common ground, it won't be too difficult to take the conversation further.

• Ask Open-Ended Questions

Did you find nothing to talk about after asking the previous questions? Don't worry; not everyone has similar interests. It's not unusual to fail to find common ground with people. Look for something else to talk about by asking open-ended questions.

o What do you like about those kinds of movies?

o Why do you like that genre of music?

o How did you feel when you stepped out into that chilly night?

o Where did you go?

o How was the food at the place you visited?

If they respond with long, elaborate answers, it implies that they are interested in taking the conversation further. However, don't be disheartened if they reply in monosyllables, like "nothing in particular," "it was okay," or "just." It may have nothing to do with you. They may just not be in the mood to talk right now, or they may be an introvert. Leave them be, or try asking open-ended questions about random things. Renowned American psychologist Arthur Aron came up with several interesting questions in a 1990s newspaper article. Here are a few that will take your conversation deeper into meaningful territory.

o What would you do if you had all the money in the world?

o Which animal would you talk with if they could understand you?

o If you were to drop dead right now, what would you most regret doing (or saying)?

o What would you rather be doing instead of talking right now?

These questions may be hypothetical, but they are quite personal. If they are uncomfortable answering any of those, don't force them to do so.

• Listen to Their Response

If they do manage to answer your open-ended questions, listen to their response. Frequently, new acquaintances make small talk just to pass the time. They don't really listen to each other, which is why the conversation eventually becomes stale. At other times, you may be hearing them out just so you can respond to something to nudge the conversation along a bit.

However, if you really listen to them without having a hidden agenda or hastening to reply, you'll realize the fruitfulness of the conversation, which will automatically lead it into meaningful waters. Use the active listening tips mentioned in the previous section. More importantly, ask follow-up questions that start with "why?"

    o Why do you like those kinds of movies?

    o Why would you talk to that animal?

    o Why would you regret doing that?

It helps you dig deeper into their psyche to understand them better so you can have a more meaningful conversation with them. "Why?" questions usually seem judgmental without meaning to. Show some genuine curiosity while asking so they don't misconstrue your intent.

• Share in Turn

A dialogue isn't a speech or a one-way conversation. That's called a monologue. A dialogue is a conversation between two or more people. It's a give-and-take mechanism. Sometimes, the other person just needs to be heard, but most of the time, they want you to share your stories, too.

Admittedly, being the center of attention may be a daunting prospect for many. Don't think about it that way. Imagine you are simply trying to recollect some forgotten dream or unearth some old memory. Assume that you are sharing it with yourself. Think that the other person is just a part of you. You have already developed a connection with them. It's time to strengthen your bond by establishing two-way communication.

You don't have to share anything personal or intimate you don't want to. Tell them something you have been through, like a funny incident or a touching story. Have you seen their favorite movie? Tell them why you liked or disliked it. A difference in opinion means you'll have more to talk about.

It's entirely possible that they haven't opened up at all despite your probing questions, but they are displaying non-verbal cues that they are interested in talking to you. That is when you should take the initiative to share first. They may be shy or afraid to speak up. Make them comfortable around you by sharing something personal. They may just feel compelled to share in turn!

• Remember FORD

FORD is an acronym popularly used by marketing professionals and business magnates to build a relationship beyond small talk with their clients. Its full form is Family, Occupation, Recreation, and Dreams. You can ease into any dialogue by asking about dreams. It isn't too personal, and if you can relate to that dream, you can discuss it with them for a long time. This is very similar to talking about occupations.

Family may be a bit personal, but you can simply ask after their spouse or children and what they are doing. Don't probe into their personal matters. Recreation is nothing but their hobbies. What do they like to do in their spare time? What kind of sports do they play? Which activities do they like to spend their time on?

• The 20-40 Seconds Talk

When you have found a common topic, are you afraid to talk about it? Alternatively, are you afraid to keep talking about it and risk boring the other person? Follow the 20-40 seconds rule. You only need to talk for 20 seconds, after which you should wrap up your side of the story within another 20 seconds. Then, ask an open-ended question to show your interest in their opinions about the topic.

These 20-40 seconds give you enough time to look for verbal and non-verbal cues to determine their level of interest in the topic. If they display negative cues, ask an open-ended question about some other topic.

Topics to Avoid

Transitioning from small talk to a meaningful conversation involves discussing topics that interest both of you. However, certain topics may breed animosity or bring negative vibes into your relationship. Stay away from discussing anything that has the potential to become controversial or blow up into an argument.

You know which topics you have strong feelings about. Don't transition into discussing those. As a general rule, you should avoid talking about religion, politics, personal problems, professional woes, health issues, controversial news, and anything sexual.

While all these topics have excellent conversational potential, they aren't exactly ideal for the transitional period and may also end your interaction on a negative note. For instance, you both love to talk about the country's political situation. However, you are a Democrat, whereas they are a Republican. You may have a healthy debate in the beginning, but it won't take long for the situation to escalate into an unhealthy argument.

First, try to discover each other with simple, non-controversial topics like books, movies, workplaces, new attractions in the city, etc. Communication gurus Kathryn Greene and Amanda Carpenter believe that starting meaningful conversations is like peeling an onion. Peel the outer layer with small talk and the second layer with simple, non-controversial topics until you reach their core and have become their friend.

Chapter 10: Moving Forward

As you may know, small talk is an acquired social skill. Nobody is a natural. Like all other skills, it should be refined and honed before you can effectively master it. In short, you should practice small talk to get better at it. Imagine you are in the elevator with someone you have met once or twice. You have all the theories and techniques of small talk in mind, and you know exactly what to do.

There is an awkward silence in that enclosed space as you pick a small talk topic and frame a set of open-ended questions in your head. However, when you open your mouth to say it all, the words stay stuck in your throat and come out as a weird croak. The silence becomes even more awkward as it stretches on until, thankfully, the lift doors open, and you dash out.

There may be many reasons why you couldn't say what was on your mind, but the primary reason is *lack of practice*. Don't find yourself in a socially awkward situation again. Here are a few effective exercises that will help you sharpen your small talk skills, like a well-sharpened blade.

Breathing and Meditation

Meditation can help relieve stress and anxiety.
https://www.pexels.com/photo/silhouette-of-man-at-daytime-1051838/

Breathing and meditation help relieve anxiety and stress. As you feel calmer, you can focus better on your small talk techniques. To practice basic meditation, breathe normally for a couple of minutes as you sit in solitude, free of distractions. Don't think of anything other than your inhalation and exhalation processes. Then, after you inhale, hold your breath and start speaking as you exhale. Say anything you are thinking of at that moment. Even a continuous "Ah" sound will do. When you have exhaled completely, stop speaking, inhale again, and repeat the exercise.

To relax quickly and more effectively before speaking, try this alternate nostril breathing exercise.

1. Hold your right nostril closed with your right thumb and breathe in through your left nostril.

2. Release the pressure on your right nostril as you hold your left one closed with your index finger.

3. Breathe out through your right nostril and breathe in again.

4. Close your right nostril as you open your left one, and repeat the process until serenity wraps you up in its warm embrace.

Journaling

Journaling is the art of writing down whatever you are feeling or thinking. It's like writing an autobiography. It helps you reflect on your decisions, good or bad, and focus on the future. Keeping a journal as you practice small talk is a great way to improve your social skills. Here are a few good journaling prompts you can use.

- **Before heading out,** imagine various social situations you may come across and note down how you can begin your small talk in each scenario. For example, you meet your neighbor in the corridor. Apart from the "hi's" and "how are you's," you can ask how they are settling in or talk about the changing weather. Make a note of that in your journal so you don't have to fish for small talk topics as you meet people.

- **Before heading out,** think about what makes you feel anxious about talking to someone. Are you worried about what they might think if you screw up? Does their talkative nature make you feel uncomfortable? Does your low self-esteem get in the way of engaging in small talk? Be true to yourself and note down the real reasons, even if they are harsh. Then, list out ways in which you can overcome them.

- **After coming back home,** make a note of all your small talk with people, excluding your conversations with close friends and family. You don't need a photographic memory. Just outline the important points, like when they commented on the dreary weather or how you assured them that it would brighten up soon.

- **After coming back home,** try to recollect all the mistakes you made during your small talk and write them down. Follow it up with what you should have said in its stead. For instance, as soon as you changed the topic, you immediately realized from their slightly crestfallen face that they wanted to pursue it. Still, you went ahead and talked about the new topic. Write down how you could have been more insightful and caring, apologized for the abrupt change, and encouraged them to speak their mind.

Mirror Talk

This activity looks exactly as the name suggests. You talk to yourself in the mirror. There is nothing wrong with talking to yourself as long as you are making sense. Mirror talk has a number of proven psychological benefits. You'll grow in your confidence to talk with others, boost your self-esteem, reduce your social anxiety, and get yourself ready for any kind of social interaction.

All you need to do is stand in front of a mirror and talk. Don't directly start practicing small talk, however. Repeat a few positive affirmations first.

- I can talk with anyone.
- I'm not afraid to talk.
- I'm confident in talking without faltering.
- I'm a wizard at making small talk.
- I'm no longer surrounded by anxious thoughts.
- Stress is slowly vanishing into thin air.
- I'll go about my day with a confident smile.

Keep repeating these affirmations (or any variations of these) until you begin to feel what they want you to feel. As your self-esteem grows, you may be raring to try your small talk techniques with strangers and acquaintances. Try them out in the mirror first. Start with a simple "Hello, how are you?" Respond to yourself, and proceed to talk about the weather. Switch to the current news or sports as you comment on your own responses. Resort to innovative ways while switching topics and make a smooth transition from small talk into meaningful conversation.

Conversation Role-Play with a Close Friend

You don't usually do small talk with close friends or family. You are already comfortable around them, and you have more important topics to discuss. This natural camaraderie is ideal for practicing and polishing your small talk skills. Set aside an hour each day with your friend for this kind of role-play. Imagine the two of you don't know each other well and meet up in different situations.

How will you start the conversation, keep it going, ease into a meaningful dialogue, and end it on a favorable note? Put all the skills you have learned so far to use during role-play, right from making a good first impression to embracing diversity and honesty. Here are a few scenarios you can imagine.

- **You Met Them in the Elevator.** Only the two of you are present, or there are already a few strangers around. Put yourself in both possible scenarios and notice whether or not you change your behavior. Ideally, you shouldn't. There's a difference between passersby on the street and strangers in an enclosed space. The latter will affect your conversation more. Practice focusing on your small talk rather than worrying about other people.

- **You Met Them on the Street.** This is the best place to talk about the weather or the traffic. You can also talk about where you or they are headed. On the street, small talk is usually short and terse because people are in a hurry. Ask your friend to attempt to end the conversation, whereas you try to keep them interested for as long as you can.

- **They Are a Workplace or a School Acquaintance.** Schools and workplaces thrive on water cooler gossip, so try to ease into it as you begin the small talk. Tell them the day feels promising to get more work done. Talk about how you were almost late because of the traffic, and ask if they faced the same problem. Then, proceed to academic or work-related topics. Two colleagues or students can keep the conversation going for hours on end with those topics.

- **You Met Them at a Party.** The small talk here will be entirely different. You don't talk about the weather or the traffic at parties, though it might be a good starting point if you're meeting someone for the first time. Don't linger on such superficial topics too long. You have to think on your feet and come up with ways to ease into an interesting dialogue. Try to find a common ground in as short a time as possible. If you are unable to find one, start talking about a recent sports game or ask an intriguing hypothetical question, like "What do you want to do before you die?"

Find the Lie

This is a group game that makes small talk more interesting as you get to know each other better. You can play it with one other individual too, but it's more fun in a group.

1. State three things about yourself, two of which are true, and one is a lie.
2. The person sitting next to you will get *one chance* to guess the lie.
3. If they guess wrong, they sit out for one round.
4. You'll continue your turn by stating three more things different from before.
5. The person next in line will try to guess.
6. If they guess it right, then all the participants can ask you questions about the true statements if they want. You'll have to answer all their questions, whether you want to or not.

Your listening skills will be vastly improved, and you can make a note of some really interesting questions to further your small talk techniques.

Questions upon Questions

Have you run out of questions to ask during small talk? This activity will help brainstorm some exciting new questions for you. Request a few friends or colleagues to participate.

1. Ask an open-ended question that initiates small talk with the person sitting beside you (whose name is, say, John).
2. They will answer and ask another question to the one sitting beside them.
3. When it's your turn again, you'll have to remember John's answer and ask a follow-up question.

This way, you can not only boost your memory but also add several new questions to your growing small talk list. To make the game more interesting and all-inclusive, you can start the second round by asking a follow-up question to the person sitting next to John. You'll have to keep track of everyone's answers because, after a few more rounds, you'll be asking John a follow-up question again!

Summarizing Audio Stories

This is a great way to improve your listening skills, the key ingredient of small talk. Nowadays, many books have been converted to audio files where a narrator reads the book out loud.

1. Pick an audiobook that contains a collection of short stories, like The Memoirs of Sherlock Holmes, and start listening to it.

2. Hit the pause button when the first story is completed.

3. Pull out your journal and write a brief summary highlighting the important points.

4. Rewind and listen to the story again. If you missed something important, make a note of it and highlight it with a different marker.

Repeat the same exercise with all the other stories. After summarizing a good 5-10 stories, you'll have greatly improved your listening skills.

Common Interests Activity

This activity not only helps you discover each other's interests but also increases your capability of asking questions.

1. Tell them to keep their favorite hobby in mind.

2. Ask a yes-or-no question regarding any hobby without specifically naming it.

3. Keep asking more questions based on their answers to guess the hobby they have in mind. Then, let them do the same with you.

For instance, you can ask, "Is it related to direction and production?" If their hobby is watching theater plays, then they will answer yes. But your first guess will probably be watching movies. You'll get it right on the second or third guess. Neither can have more than three guesses.

Keep a count of the questions. Whoever guesses right with the least number of questions wins. In the case of a large group, each person can ask only one question per round to every participant. In the next round, you need to ask a different question. The rounds will keep on adding up until every participant has guessed the hobby of every other. This is much more difficult than the one-on-one activity since you need to remember what you asked each participant after every round, but that makes it even more exciting.

Speak Only Once

Are you in the habit of interrupting people while they are talking? That is a big negative while making small talk. This activity will help you acquire that much-needed restraint.

1. Pick any broad topic (say, movies).

2. One person will ask an opinion-based question about it (say, what would you criticize about *The Godfather (1972)*?).

3. Whoever wants to speak will raise their hand. The questioner reserves the right to choose the speaker.

4. The chosen person will state their opinions and elaborate on them.

If you are a fan of the movie, you'll feel the urge to respond to the criticizing opinions. However, if you have already spoken once regarding some other question, the questioner won't allow you to talk. To raise the stakes, the person who raises their hand after they have spoken once or speaks out of turn will automatically lose the game.

Mime an Emotion

Two people can play this game, but the more, the merrier. Let one person choose an emotion. They will act it out, and you need to identify it. For example, they picked a frown and mimicked the emotion on their face. You interpreted it as anger, so you'll lose a point. This activity helps you enhance your skills of understanding body language. It also improves your ability to express yourself through body language. After you have identified every emotion, you can move on to act out different situations or real-life scenarios.

Mirror the Other

This is an exciting kid's activity that is doubly fun for adults. You need to mirror/copy every action of the other participant, down to the smallest things. For instance, if they are acting like they are throwing a ball, observe their stance and mirror the entire action. If you just made the hand action without moving your foot as they did, you'll lose the game. This activity heightens your observation so you can notice the tiniest change in their body language during small talk. Practice it enough to be able to catch any negative signs immediately, no matter how subtle they are.

Practicing Your Newly Acquired Small Talk Skills in Real-Time

Once you engage in all or most of these activities every week, you'll get used to the art of small talk. Participation by colleagues or acquaintances will be an even greater benefit. However, when you actually get down to small talk in real-time with a complete stranger, you may still not be able to talk well. Don't dive directly into the depths of the social waters.

Start small. Reconnect with a long-lost friend or someone you haven't met for a long time but had excellent relations with. Progress to acquaintances or friends of friends. Are they having a low-key party at their place? Ask if you can join them. It's a perfect, low-pressure place where barely anyone knows you, so try your skills. After that, you are bound to acquire the confidence to engage in small talk with complete strangers anywhere in the world.

Conclusion

Small talk may not be a substantial form of communication, but it paves the way for more important conversations. It's an initiation for you to determine if the other person can connect with you, like testing the water before drinking it, literally and figuratively. It's not too difficult to master once you practice all the techniques as you enjoy the activities.

In summary, consider small talk as more of an art than a social skill, then it will be easier to practice. Like every drop of paint contributes to the entire masterpiece, small talk leads you to a more compelling and wholesome conversation. The best part is that you don't need a strong creative side to understand and put it into practice. People from all walks of life can master the art of small talk.

Nail your first impressions. They have a lasting impact on people's minds. Your non-verbal body language plays a major role in making a good first impression, and so does your authentic and frank nature. If you made a bad first impression, you don't have to worry. Anybody's perception of you can be changed with time. The most crucial factor that influences this change is your ability to listen.

While listening, you not only hear what they are saying but also understand and acknowledge their speech. You can act as if you are actively listening, but it's hard work. It's much easier to develop a genuine interest in the person so you can actively listen to them for real.

Honesty matters in any relationship, and small talk is no different, but don't be brutally honest. Let your genuine personality shine, but don't overshare. If your personality doesn't include diversity, learn that trait.

Small talk is a universal language, and unless you can communicate with a diverse audience, you won't be able to master it. It also includes body language.

Your smallest gestures and tiniest variations in posture can speak volumes about your personality. These non-verbal cues are a small talk language all of its own. However, don't let that make you anxious. Stress and anxiety are major hurdles to improving your communication skills. Understand their core nature and get rid of them using therapeutic techniques. Only then will you be able to small-talk your way into professional success.

The final step to mastering the art is to steer it toward a meaningful, substantial conversation. This transition should be smooth and seamless so that it doesn't bring awkwardness into the situation and ruin your small talk effort. The ultimate lesson is to never join the fray without proper preparation. You need a lot of practice with many fun activities!

Here's another book by Andy Gardner that you might like

Free Bonus from Andy Gardner

Hi!

My name is Andy Gardner, and first off, I want to THANK YOU for reading my book.

Now you have a chance to join my exclusive email list related to human psychology and self-development so you can get the ebook below for free as well as the potential to get more ebooks for free! Simply click the link below to join.

P.S. Remember that it's 100% free to join the list.

Access your free bonuses here:
https://livetolearn.lpages.co/andy-gardner-small-talk-paperback/

References

(N.d.). Indeed.com. https://www.indeed.com/career-advice/career-development/how-to-make-small-talks

(N.d.-a). Masterclass.com. https://www.masterclass.com/articles/how-to-use-active-listening-to-improve-your-communication-skills

(N.d.-b). Indeed.com. https://www.indeed.com/career-advice/career-development/passive-vs-active-listening

Acceptance and commitment therapy. (n.d.). Psychology Today. https://www.psychologytoday.com/za/therapy-types/acceptance-and-commitment-therapy

Agbanyo, G. K., & Wang, Y. (2022). Understanding cross-cultural differences in conceptualizing international trade patterns: A neuroeconomic perspective. Frontiers in Neuroscience, 16. https://doi.org/10.3389/fnins.2022.916084

Agius, A. (2023, January 9). 12 crucial strategies for promoting team collaboration — plus, the biggest collaboration roadblocks, according to ClickUp's CEO. HubSpot. https://blog.hubspot.com/service/team-collaboration

And, C. (n.d.). Cultural Sensitivity. Nyc.gov. https://www.nyc.gov/assets/ochia/downloads/pdf/cultural_sensitivity_wkshp.pdf

Anderson, A. (2021, November 22). 9 steps to mastering the art of small talk. The British School of Excellence. https://thebritishschoolofexcellence.com/life-skills/9-steps-to-mastering-the-art-of-small-talk/

ApS, N. (2021, September 22). 7 tips to improve your active listening skills [with examples]. Novorésumé; Novorésumé ApS. https://novoresume.com/career-blog/active-listening

Arlin Cuncic, M. (2023, February 16). 10 Best and Worst Small Talk Topics. Verywell Mind.

https://www.verywellmind.com/small-talk-topics-3024421#:~:text=What%20is%20the%20purpose%20of,in%20line%20at%20the%20store.

Arlin Cuncic, M. A. (2017, September 5). Coping with social anxiety stigma. Verywell Mind. https://www.verywellmind.com/coping-with-social-anxiety-stigma-4149499

Bilefsky, D. (2020, October 5). In Canada, Kamala Harris, a disco-dancing teenager, yearned for home. The New York Times.

Body Language Activities. (n.d.). Enableireland.Ie. https://enableireland.ie/sites/default/files/publication/Body%20Language%20Activities.pdf

Bowe, J. (2021, August 17). People who are good at small talk always avoid these 7 mistakes, says public speaking expert. CNBC. https://www.cnbc.com/2021/08/17/avoid-these-mistakes-if-you-want-to-be-good-at-small-talk-says-public-speaking-expert.html

Breathe and speak with ease – THE VOICE FOUNDATION. (2013, August 26). THE VOICE FOUNDATION – Advancing Understanding of the Voice Through Interdisciplinary Research & Education; THE VOICE FOUNDATION. https://voicefoundation.org/articles/breathe-and-speak-with-ease/

Brown, D. (2017, August 20). How one man convinced 200 Ku Klux Klan members to give up their robes. NPR. https://www.npr.org/2017/08/20/544861933/how-one-man-convinced-200-ku-klux-klan-members-to-give-up-their-robes

Brown, K. (2022, September 22). 6 ways to stop oversharing and talking too much. Science of People. https://www.scienceofpeople.com/stop-oversharing/

Cherry, K. (2023, August 23). 8 tips for starting a conversation. Verywell Mind. https://www.verywellmind.com/how-to-start-a-conversation-4582339#toc-prepare-ahead-of-time

Collins, H. K., Hagerty, S. F., & Quoidbach, J. (2022, October 17). Relational diversity in social portfolios predicts well-being. Relational Diversity in Social Portfolios Predicts Well-Being – Article – Faculty & Research – Harvard Business School. https://www.hbs.edu/faculty/Pages/item.aspx?num=62955

Cronkleton, E. (2019, April 9). 10 breathing exercises to try: For stress, training, and lung capacity. Healthline. https://www.healthline.com/health/breathing-exercise

Dayton, L. (2010, September 13). Social Support Network may add to longevity. Los Angeles Times. https://www.latimes.com/health/la-xpm-2010-sep-13-la-he-friends-health-20100913-story.html

Endrass, B., Nakano, Y., Lipi, A. A., Rehm, M., & André, E. (2011). Culture-related topic selection in small talk conversations across Germany and Japan. In Intelligent Virtual Agents (pp. 1–13). Springer Berlin Heidelberg.

Epley, N., & Schroeder, J. (2014). Mistakenly seeking solitude. Journal of Experimental Psychology: General, 143(5), 1980–1999. https://doi.org/10.1037/a0037323

First Impressions. (n.d.). Psychology Today. https://www.psychologytoday.com/us/basics/first-impressions

Flaherty, M. (n.d.). My favorite Nelson Mandela (mis)quote. Harvard.edu. https://scholar.harvard.edu/pierredegalbert/node/632263

Forscher, P. S., Mitamura, C., Dix, E. L., Cox, W. T. L., & Devine, P. G. (2017). Breaking the prejudice habit: Mechanisms, timecourse, and longevity. Journal of Experimental Social Psychology, 72, 133–146. https://doi.org/10.1016/j.jesp.2017.04.009

Foulkes, L. (2021, April 28). How to have more meaningful conversations. Psyche; Psyche Magazine. https://psyche.co/guides/how-to-have-more-meaningful-conversations

fromExploreWithDora, M. (n.d.). Finding common interests in class activity. TPT. https://www.teacherspayteachers.com/Product/Finding-Common-Interests-Class-Activity-10203808?st=dc594ff6321fa175ac769fe2ffb4c538

Frost, A. (2023, October 12). The Ultimate Guide to Small Talk: Conversation Starters, Powerful Questions, & More. HubSpot Blog. https://blog.hubspot.com/sales/small-talk-guide#:~:text=It%20doesn't%20matter%20how,skill%20just%20like%20any%20other.

Gerber, S. (2019, May 5). 7 hand gesture body language tips to influence communication. Sandygerber.com; Sandy Gerber. https://sandygerber.com/7-hand-gesture-body-language-tips-to-influence-communication/

Gould, W. R. (2021, July 22). Why vulnerability in relationships is so important. Verywell Mind. https://www.verywellmind.com/why-vulnerability-in-relationships-is-so-important-5193728

Grant, R. (n.d.). More Than Handshakes: What is Professional Networking? Snhu.edu. https://www.snhu.edu/about-us/newsroom/career/value-of-professional-networking

Harden, C. (2018, March 20). Mike (social anxiety). Society of Clinical Psychology | Division 12 of the American Psychological Association; Society of Clinical Psychology. https://div12.org/case_study/mike-social-anxiety/

Harris, T. R. (2018, April 11). 5 quick tips to overcome the fear of talking to someone. The Exceptional Skills. https://www.theexceptionalskills.com/tips-overcome-fear-talking-someone/

Haugan, T. (2023). Social anxiety in modern societies from an evolutionary perspective. Discover Psychology, 3(1). https://doi.org/10.1007/s44202-023-00074-6

Haupt, A. (2023, June 1). 7 ways to get better at small talk—and why you should. Time. https://time.com/6280607/small-talk-tips-benefits/

Higuera, V. (2012, July 2). Social anxiety disorder. Healthline. https://www.healthline.com/health/anxiety/social-phobia

How to be truthful without being hurtful. (2019, February 13). Psychology Today. https://www.psychologytoday.com/za/blog/your-emotional-meter/201902/how-be-truthful-without-being-hurtful

Hur, J., DeYoung, K. A., Islam, S., Anderson, A. S., Barstead, M. G., & Shackman, A. J. (2020). Social context and the real-world consequences of social anxiety. Psychological Medicine, 50(12), 1989–2000. https://doi.org/10.1017/s0033291719002022

Jamsa, P. (2019, June 5). 5 ways how journaling can help you to overcome social anxiety. Succeed in Your Career. https://succeedinyourcareer.com/5-ways-how-journaling-can-help-you-to-get-over-social-anxiety/

Jefferson, J. W. (2001). Social anxiety disorder: More than just a little shyness. The Primary Care Companion to CNS Disorders, 3(1), 4. https://doi.org/10.4088/pcc.v03n0102

Jensen, V. L., Hougaard, E., & Fishman, D. B. (2013). Part 1: The case of "Sara" Sara, a social phobia client with sudden change after exposure exercises in intensive cognitive-behavior group therapy: A case-based analysis of mechanisms of change. Pragmatic Case Studies in Psychotherapy: PCSP, 9(3), 275–336. https://psycnet.apa.org/fulltext/2013-38429-001.pdf

Jongman-Sereno, K. P., & Leary, M. R. (2019). The enigma of being yourself: A critical examination of the concept of authenticity. Review of General Psychology: Journal of Division 1, of the American Psychological Association, 23(1), 133–142. https://doi.org/10.1037/gpr0000157

Korn, J. (2022, November 9). Why small talk is anything but small. Forbes. https://www.forbes.com/sites/juliawuench/2021/06/21/why-small-talk-is-anything-but-small/?sh=75581515f78b0

Lai, F., Wang, L., Zhang, J., Shan, S., Chen, J., & Tian, L. (2023). Relationship between social media use and social anxiety in college students: Mediation effect of communication capacity. International Journal of Environmental Research and Public Health, 20(4), 3657. https://doi.org/10.3390/ijerph20043657

Lerner, J. S., Li, Y., Valdesolo, P., & Kassam, K. S. (2015). Emotion and decision making. Annual Review of Psychology, 66(1), 799–823. https://doi.org/10.1146/annurev-psych-010213-115043

Marie, S. (2016, May 17). Vulnerability in relationships: Benefits and tips. Psych Central. https://psychcentral.com/relationships/trust-and-vulnerability-in-relationships

Martin, T. (2022, April 20). 7 engaging listening activities for small groups. Esparklearning.com. https://www.esparklearning.com/blog/7-engaging-listening-activities-for-small-groups/

McAleer, P., Todorov, A., & Belin, P. (2014). How do you say "hello"? Personality impressions from brief novel voices. PloS One, 9(3), e90779. https://doi.org/10.1371/journal.pone.0090779

MindTools. (n.d.). Mindtools.com. https://www.mindtools.com/az4wxv7/active-listening

MindTools. (n.d.). Mindtools.com. https://www.mindtools.com/aejizul/body-language

Molinsky, A., & Hahn, M. (2015, April 8). Building relationships in cultures that don't do small talk. Harvard Business Review. https://hbr.org/2015/04/building-relationships-in-cultures-that-dont-do-small-talk

Netburn, D. (2023, January 3). Why talking to strangers is good for your mental health. Los Angeles Times. https://www.latimes.com/california/newsletter/2023-01-03/why-talking-to-strangers-is-good-for-your-mental-health-group-therapy

Nonverbal communication and body language – Helpguide.org. (n.d.). https://www.helpguide.org/articles/relationships-communication/nonverbal-communication.htm

Nova Scotia, D. (2023, October 6). Small talk matters more than you think. Doctors Nova Scotia. https://www.yourdoctors.ca/blog/healthy-living/small-talk

Parsons, L. (2022, December 16). How to build business relationships. Professional Development | Harvard DCE. https://professional.dce.harvard.edu/blog/how-to-build-business-relationships/

Perry, E. (n.d.). How to carry a conversation — the art of making connections. Betterup.com. https://www.betterup.com/blog/how-to-carry-a-conversation

Ro, T. (2019, May 1). How to turn small talk into smart conversation. Remote Symfony Team. https://medium.com/remote-symfony-team/how-to-turn-small-talk-into-smart-conversation-d3b44ba6e962

Sandstrom, Gillian & Dunn, Elizabeth. (2014). Is Efficiency Overrated?. Social Psychological and Personality Science. 5. 437-442. 10.1177/1948550613502990.

Schab, F. (2018, January 18). The Psychology of First Impressions. Six Degrees. https://www.six-degrees.com/the-psychology-of-first-impressions/

Selby. (2023, August 19). Fun and Effective Small Talk Activities for developing social skills. Everyday Speech. https://everydayspeech.com/sel-implementation/fun-and-effective-small-talk-activities-for-developing-social-skills/

Selby. (2023, August 19). How to Show Genuine Interest in a conversation: Enhancing your communication skills. Everyday Speech. https://everydayspeech.com/sel-implementation/how-to-show-genuine-interest-in-a-conversation-enhancing-your-communication-skills/

Social anxiety disorder (social phobia). (2021, June 19). Mayo Clinic. https://www.mayoclinic.org/diseases-conditions/social-anxiety-disorder/symptoms-causes/syc-20353561

South Palomares, J. K., & Young, A. W. (2018). Facial first impressions of partner preference traits: Trustworthiness, status, and attractiveness. Social Psychological and Personality Science, 9(8), 990–1000. https://doi.org/10.1177/1948550617732388

Sprabary, A. (2022, July 6). How important is eye contact in communication? All About Vision. https://www.allaboutvision.com/resources/human-interest/importance-of-eye-contact

Stern, J. (1478525332000). Why professional networking is so important. Linkedin.com. https://www.linkedin.com/pulse/why-professional-networking-so-important-jordan-parikh

Sutton, J. (2016, July 21). Active listening: The art of empathetic conversation. Positivepsychology.com. https://positivepsychology.com/active-listening/

Sutton, J. (2020, August 27). What is intuition and why is it important? 5 examples. Positivepsychology.com. https://positivepsychology.com/intuition/

The First Impression Bias. (2021, December 14). The Decision Lab. https://thedecisionlab.com/reference-guide/psychology/the-first-impression-bias

The Power of First Impressions: Building Trust and Connections. (n.d.). Linkedin.Com. https://www.linkedin.com/pulse/power-first-impressions-building-trust-connections-anuj-mahajan/?trk=article-ssr-frontend-pulse_more-articles_related-content-card

The Psychology of First Impressions. (2017, October 3). Imagine Health. https://imaginehealth.ie/psychology-first-impressions/

The SuperHERO Teacher Brittany Wheaton. (2020, February 15). Using mirror talk to spark growth mindset, positivity, and confidence in students. The SuperHERO Teacher. https://thesuperheroteacher.com/2020/02/using-mirror-talk-to-spark-growth-mindset-positivity-and-confidence-in-students.html

The surprising benefits of being yourself. (n.d.). Psychology Today. https://www.psychologytoday.com/za/blog/fulfillment-any-age/202110/the-surprising-benefits-being-yourself

Williams, R. (2019, February 11). The Psychology of First Impressions: Are They Accurate? Ray Williams. https://raywilliams.ca/psychology-first-impressions-accurate/

Young Entrepreneur Council. (2014, July 22). 17 tips to survive your next networking event. Forbes. https://www.forbes.com/sites/yec/2014/07/22/17-tips-to-survive-your-next-networking-event/?sh=140d16817cd4

Zigomo, T. (n.d.). Friendship & authenticity at work in professional and managerial women in South African organisations. Wits.Ac.Za. https://wiredspace.wits.ac.za/server/api/core/bitstreams/0047c636-bf84-4c29-954e-4910c9983e5f/content